TWENTIETH CENTURY
INTERPRETATIONS

MAYNARD MACK, *Series Editor*
Yale University

NOW AVAILABLE
Collections of Critical Essays
ON

TWENTIETH CENTURY INTERPRETATIONS
OF
SIR GAWAIN
AND THE
GREEN KNIGHT

TWENTIETH CENTURY INTERPRETATIONS
OF

SIR GAWAIN
AND THE
GREEN KNIGHT

A Collection of Critical Essays

Edited by
DENTON FOX

Prentice-Hall, Inc. *Englewood Cliffs, N. J.*
A SPECTRUM BOOK

Contents

SIR GAWAIN
AND THE
GREEN KNIGHT

Introduction

by Denton Fox

It is striking that the three greatest Middle English poets were almost exact contemporaries. Chaucer died in 1400; his poems were written between 1365 and 1400. The three versions of *Piers Plowman*, which are almost certainly all the work of William Langland, are usually dated between 1365 and 1399, although we do not know Langland's dates. We know neither the dates nor the name of the author of *Sir Gawain and the Green Knight*, but the poem must have been written sometime during the last part of the fourteenth century: it is usually assigned to the periods 1360–1400 or 1375–1400.

While it is surely not a simple coincidence that so much great poetry was written during the same decades, it would be impossible to unravel all the multitudinous causes for this extraordinary outburst. But there is one cause which is both important and clear: the establishment of English as a respectable language. Norman French had never been spoken by more than a minority of Englishmen, but it had been, in theory if not always in practice, the proper language of the upper class. So a poet who wished to write for an aristocratic (and therefore remunerative) audience would write in French, while a loftier-minded poet who wished his work to survive in future time, and to circulate outside of his own particular part of England, would write either in French or, very often, in Latin. But during the thirteenth and fourteenth centuries English was slowly displacing French. While this was a very gradual process, it is interesting that in 1362 English was officially accepted in two important ways: parliament was opened, for the first time, with a speech in English, and a statute was enacted that all lawsuits should be pleaded and judged in English.[1]

For a serious poet in the last part of the fourteenth century, then, English was a language lying open and ready to be used. But because

[1] See A. C. Baugh, *A History of the English Language,* Second ed. (New York: Appleton-Century-Crofts, 1957), pp. 176–78.

the traditions of English verse had been to some degree submerged after the Norman conquest, and had fared differently in different parts of England, it would not have been obvious to an observer living in the middle of the century just how English would be used by future poets. A glance at the divergent paths chosen by Chaucer, Langland, and the Gawain-poet will show how various the possibilities were.

Metrically, Chaucer followed and in part developed what was to be the main line of English verse. His early poems are in octosyllabic couplets, a form mostly French in origin which had already become naturalized, but the bulk of his work is in iambic pentameter, a line which had not been used before, in any important way, in English, but which was to become the most standard English meter. Linguistically, Chaucer was also in what was to be the central tradition: his dialect was essentially London English, which is in most respects the basis of modern standard English. Chaucer's matter is too variegated for easy generalizations, but it is in many ways both modern and continental: one obvious indication of this is that a large proportion of his plots are drawn from fourteenth-century French and Italian writers.

Langland and the Gawain-poet both belong, of course, to the native alliterative tradition, and so metrically their links are with the past and not with the future. The facts about the Middle English alliterative tradition are well known, if somewhat baffling. With the major exception of Layamon's *Brut,* and the minor exception of a handful of scraps, no alliterative verse survives from the beginning of the Middle English period (*c.* 1080) until about 1350. But at that time there began the so-called "Alliterative Revival," and there survive a number of alliterative poems which were written during the next century and a half, mostly by poets living in western or northern England, or in Scotland. These poems vary widely in quality, in subject matter, and even in meter: some of them, like *Gawain,* are in stanzas of one sort or another. But they all clearly have, for their metrical ancestor, the Anglo-Saxon alliterative line. Presumably, alliterative poetry continued to flourish between 1080 and 1350, but has, for the most part, not survived from this period, whether because of destruction of manuscripts, or because it was never written down in the first place. The term "Alliterative Revival," then, is at best an exaggeration: it is not that a dead tradition came to life, but that after 1350 a living and changing tradition took on new strength, like the English language itself.

Piers Plowman and *Gawain,* however, are very dissimilar poems,

despite their common roots. Two short quotations, the first from
Piers and the second from *Gawain,* may throw into relief some of their
distinctive qualities.

And alle the wyse that euere were by auȝte I can aspye,
Preysen pouerte for best lyf if pacience it folwe,
And bothe bettere and blisseder by many folde than ricchesse.
Al though it be soure to suffre there cometh swete after;
As on a walnot with-oute is a bitter barke . . .

He lyȝtes luflych adoun, leuez his corsour,
Braydez out a bryȝt bront and bigly forth strydez,
Foundez fast þurȝ þe forth þer þe felle bydez.
Þe wylde watz war of þe wyȝe with weppen in honde,
Hef hyȝly þe here, so hetterly he fnast . . .²

In both of these passages one can discern the basic pattern of the
Anglo-Saxon alliterative line, which was made up of two half-lines,
each with two stresses, bound together by alliteration between some
of the stressed syllables. In both passages, also, though especially
in the one from *Piers,* it is apparent that the regular Old English
pattern has become loosened; this loosening, already apparent in some
late Old English poetry, is a normal characteristic of fourteenth and
fifteenth-century alliterative verse. So here some half-lines seem to
have three stresses instead of two, and, in the passage from *Piers,* the
two halves of a full line are not always bound together by allitera-
tion.³

The most obvious difference between the two passages is simply that
the lines from *Gawain* need a translation, while the lines from
Piers are reasonably transparent. In part, this may come from a
difference in dialect. Langland's own dialect is uncertain, but he

²*Piers the Plowman,* ed. W. W. Skeat (London: Oxford University Press, 1886),
B. XI. 247–51. *Sir Gawain and the Green Knight,* ed. J. R. R. Tolkien and E. V.
Gordon, Second ed., rev. by Norman Davis (Oxford: Clarendon Press, 1967), ll.
1583–87 ("He dismounts gracefully, leaves his courser, draws out a bright sword
and strides forth mightily, hastens quickly through the stream where the fierce
one waits. The wild beast was aware of the man with weapon in hand; he lifted
erect his hair, so fiercely he snorted . . .").

³ The best analysis of the versification of *Gawain* is in Marie Borroff, *Sir Gawain
and the Green Knight: A Stylistic and Metrical Study* (New Haven and London:
Yale University Press, 1962); a good short account is included in her translation, *Sir
Gawain and the Green Knight* (New York: W. W. Norton and Company, Inc., 1967).

probably lived in Oxfordshire, Worcestershire, and London; his dialect was certainly closer to Chaucer's, and to ours, than was the
dialect of the Gawain-poet, who lived in the northwest Midlands. But
this accounts for only a small part of the difficulty of *Gawain's* language. A much more important factor is that the author of *Gawain*
followed, albeit with much freedom and originality, a tradition of
elevated poetic diction which goes back to Old English verse. The style
of *Gawain*, like the style of some Old English poetry, might be called
"aristocratic," not because it was necessarily intended for an audience
of aristocrats, but because it was written in a sophisticated style far
removed from the language of common speech, and because it pre-
supposes readers or listeners already trained in understanding such
verse. *Piers Plowman*, on the other hand, while by no means a simple
poem, has difficulties that come not from its language but from the
complexities of Langland's thought. One has the feeling, when reading
the two poems, that the author of *Gawain* is using with immense skill
all the resources of a traditional poetic language, as well as of colloquial speech, in order to produce precisely the effect he wishes, but
that Langland is struggling to say as clearly and vividly as possible
what is almost inexpressible. There is also very obviously a corresponding difference between the subjects of the two poems: the Gawain-poet
looks back to the traditional matter of Britain and to the time when
King Arthur was young, whereas Langland is explicitly concerned with
the immediate social, political, and religious issues of his time.

The difference between the two poems shows itself clearly in their
meters. *Gawain* is composed in conspicuously end-stopped stanzas, and
the two halves of its long alliterative lines are often carefully balanced
against each other. Many of the half-lines are formulaic, or semi-
formulaic, as in Old English poetry: "Braydez out a bryȝbront," for
instance, appears with minor changes twice elsewhere in the poem.
In *Piers Plowman* the alliterative form is much less obtrusive, and
Langland often seems to use it simply as a ready vehicle for what he
wants to say. The verse of *Piers Plowman*, unlike that of Gawain,
seems a possible forerunner of blank verse.

Of all English poets, the author of *Gawain* is perhaps the one most
badly cheated by history. Both the *Canterbury Tales* and *Piers Plowman* survive in more than fifty manuscripts, and they must have been
read by a great many men in the fifteenth and sixteenth centuries.
Gawain survives in a single small and unhandsome manuscript, and
there is no evidence to suggest that the poem ever found many readers

before it first appeared in print in 1839. While it may be partly by chance that the poem survives in only one manuscript, it may be, too, that even in the fifteenth century there were few people interested in a poem as sophisticated and as apparently old-fashioned as *Gawain*: certainly most of the surviving fifteenth-century romances are very much cruder, and obviously intended for an altogether different audience. The element of chance is perhaps more responsible for the poem having survived at all: the manuscript luckily escaped the fire which seriously damaged the Cottonian library in 1731.

It is important, however, not to imagine the author of *Gawain* to be a backwoodsman, a gifted but secluded provincial who followed the ways of his fathers because they were all he knew. He certainly lived far from London, probably in southeast Cheshire or in northeast Staffordshire, near north Wales.[4] But his audience was presumably drawn from the wealthy and cosmopolitan Lancastrian nobility, and it has been suggested several times that he may, like Chaucer, have been in the service of John of Gaunt, the duke of Lancaster. There is no reason to suppose that he was at all isolated from the European intellectual or literary currents of his times.

It is also important, I think, to remember that the author of *Gawain* must not have been, in any ordinary sense of the term, a professional composer of romances, and that *Gawain* itself is very unlike the other Middle English romances. It is sometimes called the best of these romances, but the term could, with almost equal justice, be applied to *Troilus and Criseyde* or (if it were not for the date) even to the *Faerie Queene*. A hero whose only martial exploit of any importance is to chop off a proffered head at the beginning of the poem, and whose only amorous exploit is to refuse a lady's offer of love, is in startling contrast to the typical hero of a Middle English romance.

The surviving manuscript of *Gawain* itself suggests that the poem belongs not among romances but among poetry of a very different kind. The manuscript contains, besides *Gawain*, three other poems, all in the same handwriting. The first of them is *Pearl*, a poem as beautiful and as complicated as *Gawain*, and, like it, hard to describe simply: it is partly an elegy for a dead child, partly a dialogue leading to spiritual enlightenment, and partly a vision of heaven. The other

---

[4] Professor Angus McIntosh, in "A New Approach to Middle English Dialectology," *English Studies*, XLIV (1963), 5–6, reports that the dialect of the poem, in its surviving manuscript, can be localized in this area. As he remarks, this location fits very well with the suggestions made by R. W. V. Elliott, in the article reprinted below.

two are *Purity* (sometimes called *Cleanness*) and *Patience,* both very good but lesser poems which use biblical stories in order to extol and to inculcate a virtue. Besides the evidence of the single manuscript and the common dialect, there are many stylistic, metrical, and thematic interconnections among the poems, and it is usually accepted that they are all the work of the same poet. This assumption seems proper; it is also very proper that we are reminded at intervals by various scholars that there is no real proof of a common authorship. The question is perhaps not a crucial one, since the author of *Gawain* must, at the very least, have been a man with much the same knowledge, inclinations, and inheritance as the author or authors of the other poems.[5]

In *Gawain,* as in *Pearl, Purity,* and *Patience,* the emphasis is not so much on action as on states of mind and moral problems. Where in *Purity* and *Patience* narratives were taken from the Bible and used to show the nature of a virtue, the author of *Gawain* looked to the romances to find a narrative which he could bend to his purposes. Precisely where he looked, however, is a difficult and much debated question: a large proportion of the modern scholarship on *Gawain* has been spent on a search for sources. The difficulty is that the poem combines two actions—Gawain's agreement to trade blows with the Green Knight, and his temptation by Bercilak's wife. Behind these actions lie a number of common folk-tale motifs: "the exchange of blows," "the beheading game," "the returning head," "the imperious host," "the exchange of winnings," "Potiphar's wife." And analogues for each of the two main actions can be found in earlier romances; there exist fairly close parallels for the first action, in particular.[6] But no work has been found earlier than *Gawain* in which the two actions both appear. While it is possible that the poet was following a source which has been lost, it seems very likely that he himself was responsible for joining the two actions. Certainly the combination is beautifully adapted to his purposes, since both parts are essentially tests of

---

[5] *St. Erkenwald,* an alliterative saint's legend, has sometimes also been attributed to the author of *Gawain,* on the basis of internal evidence, but it seems very unlikely that this attribution is correct. See Larry D. Benson, "The Authorship of *St. Erkenwald,*" *Journal of English and Germanic Philology,* LXIV (1965), 393–405.

[6] The most extensive account of the analogues and possible sources of *Gawain* is G. L. Kittredge, *A Study of Gawain and the Green Knight* (Cambridge, Mass.: Harvard University Press, 1916). But see also the first chapter of Larry D. Benson, *Art and Tradition in Sir Gawain and the Green Knight* (New Brunswick, N. J.: Rutgers University Press, 1965).

Gawain's fidelity, and in each test he is lured by instinctive desires—self-preservation or sexuality—to break his word, yet the two tests are also complementary: one is a public test of physical courage, the other a private and moral test.

In recent years an immense amount of criticism of the poem has been published, and the results of the different critics have been so spectacularly diverse that they put one in mind of the blind men who tried to describe an elephant. *Gawain* has been variously thought to be an historical allegory, a vegetation or solar myth, a satire on romances, an attack on the degradation of Arthur and his court, or simply an entertainment. There has been equally wild disagreement about the nature of particular characters: Bercilak, for instance, has been taken as a devil, a friendly guide, a fertility deity, and even as the Word of God. But the very fact of this confusion may suggest some of the essential qualities of the poem.

It seems safe to say, first, that the poem is not an allegory, in any simple sense of the term. Bercilak, as a supernatural creature tempting Gawain to sin, has elements of a devil; as a genial host who leads Gawain to self-knowledge, he is a friendly guide; and as a green man who dies in the winter and is miraculously reborn, he has elements of a fertility deity. But he cannot be flatly equated with any of these figures without falsifying his complexity. Another way of stating substantially the same thing would be to say that the poem is not a puzzle which one can solve if one finds the right key or the right trick. An example of this fruitless approach would be the attempts which have been made to deal with Morgain la Fée. Bercilak, at the end of the poem, remarks that she is the old woman in his castle, and that she sent him to test the pride of Arthur's knights and to grieve Guinevere. Scholars, bothered by this late-revealed motivation, have suggested that the poem goes back to a version which centered on the relationship between Gawain and a fairy-mistress, or that Morgain is both the old woman and Bercilak's wife. But theories like these do not help; they either distract one away from the poem or imply that the poet has blunderingly obscured his meaning. It seems important to take the poem as far as possible at its face value: in this instance, there is no reason to suspect that Morgain, notoriously a malign enchantress who is hostile to Arthur and his knights, is anything else than a character added by the poet to motivate the plot and to clear Bercilak himself of any guilt.

The poem is unusually solid and opaque—so much so that it is easy to look at it and see only one's own reflection. The author borrowed from the romances their objectivity and impersonality, although he spends many more lines in description, and many less in narration of action. We seldom see directly into a character's mind: Gawain's dismal night on the eve of his expected decapitation is described, for instance, either in terms of natural details, such as "Þe snawe snitered ful snart" ("The snow shivered down full bitterly"), or in terms of Gawain's behavior:

> Þe leude lystened ful wel þat leȝ in his bedde,
> Þaȝ he lowkez his liddez, ful lyttel he slepes . . .

(Lines 2006–7. "Full well the man listened who lay in his bed, though he shuts his eyelids, he sleeps very little . . .")

From his style, the poet seems like Bercilak himself: jovial, prodigious, bustling, and thoroughly inscrutable. And this effect is increased by the stanzaic form itself, in which the long alliterative lines are brought to a sharp conclusion by the disyllabic bob, and then the matter of the stanza is rolled up, often with an air of triumphant finality, in the four short rhyming lines of the wheel.

But the structure and the themes of the poem are clear enough—many of the themes are brought out even in the first stanza. The poem begins, as it ends, with a reference to the archetypal civilization of Troy, and Britain is shown as the youngest descendant and reincarnation of this civilization. But civilization is described as something fragile and mutable, threatened on one hand by the "tresoun" and "tricherie" which destroyed Troy, and on the other hand by the natural ebb and flow of "werre and wrake and wonder" ("war and distress and marvel"), or of "blysse and blunder." Throughout the stanza the emphasis is on alternation, and the verbal phrase of the last line, "Ful skete hatz skyfted" ("Full quickly has alternated"), might be taken as expressing both the structural method of the poem—the alternation between contrasting scenes—and some of its most important themes—mutability, and the interplay between nature and civilization.

In the opening scene, Arthur and his court are shown celebrating, in the most civilized way possible, the Christmas holidays. The emphasis is on joyous ceremony: the people follow, with great mirth and courtesy, traditional and even artificial customs. The atmosphere is predominantly that of youthfulness and untried innocence; all the people are in their "first age." When the Green Knight bursts in, it is as if the walls which surrounded and protected the court had suddenly been destroyed: a token of this is that the Green Knight rides his horse straight to the table. This is the first of the many tests of the poem, for here ceremony and civilization, which have temporarily ground to an appalled halt, must find a way to deal with something that is violent, natural, and inescapable. When the challenge is at last taken up by Gawain, who thereby becomes the representative of the court, it is notable that he begins by making a long, formal, and extremely courteous speech. If he had instead descended to the Green Knight's own level of natural violence, he would already have failed the test, since he would have admitted that civilized courtesy was no more than a trinket, and that it must be abandoned in an emergency.

Gawain accepts the challenge by promising to attempt to find the Green Knight in a year's time, so that he may receive a return blow: "And þat I swere þe for soþe, and by my seker traweþ" ("And that I ᵛᵉar to you truly, and by my steadfast fidelity"). This promise, and the later promises which Gawain gives when he agrees to exchange a day's winnings with Bercilak, are crucial to the plot of the poem, and also to its meaning. Hannah Arendt has some enlightening pages on the nature of promises in her *The Human Condition*. She refers to Nietzsche, who "saw in the faculty of promises . . . the very distinction which marks off human from animal life," and shows how promises give men, who would otherwise be carried along helplessly in the flux of the world, some control over the future by providing "isolated islands of certainty in an ocean of uncertainty"; she shows, also, how mutual promise has always been taken to be the foundation of civilized society.[7] So Gawain, when he performs the unnatural and apparently absurd action of going into a dead land, in a dead season, to seek his own death, is in fact asserting the possibility of meaningful human action and of an enduring civilization.

But before Gawain departs from Arthur's court, the narrative is interrupted by two complementary passages. The first is the famous and beautiful description of the seasons of the year, in which the stress is on the mutability of the world and on the inevitable alternation between life and death—"al rypez and rotez" ("everything ripens and rots"). The natural world here is shown not as hostile, since there is summer as well as winter, and not as chaotic, since the cycle of the seasons is regular, but simply as "other." Like the Green Knight himself, nature is inhuman, ever-changing, and unavoidable.

[7] Hannah Arendt, *The Human Condition* (Chicago: University of Chicago Press, 1958), pp. 243–47.

The second passage is the description of the pentangle or five-pointed star on Gawain's shield, the "endeles knot . . . of pure golde," and the explanation of its significance. Like the seasons, the pentangle is inhuman, but it is above and not below the human level, since it represents a more than earthly perfection. It is the symbol of a supernatural and explicitly Christian stability and virtue: on the obverse of the shield is the other side of the same concept, a picture of the Virgin. And it is, of course, important that the pentangle is on a shield: Gawain's protection against the natural world is his faith and virtue.

Bercilak's castle, like Alcinous's palace in the *Odyssey,* is the magical quintessence of civilization, a place where the hero is tested, not against monsters and physical perils, but against interior dangers—interior both in the sense that they are represented by domestic situations, and in the sense that the dangers are really within the hero's mind. The nature of the castle is expressed when the poet says that it looked as if it were "pared out of papure," made out of cut-paper, an image which expresses beautifully the splendor and regularity of its battlements, but also an image which suggests an insubstantial simulacrum.

Within the castle, the emphasis is entirely on courtesy. Although the people of the castle are conspicuously well-mannered and aristocratic, they rejoice because they have in Gawain a noted authority who can teach them the very finest points of courteous behavior. During Gawain's stay at the castle, his courtesy is constantly tested, and the concept of courtesy is discussed, analyzed, and finally, by implication, defined. Bercilak's wife has, or pretends to have, a definition of courtesy which is not very far from the usual modern use of the term: she thinks that courtesy consists in elegant and sophisticated manners, and that it is only an outward form. She continually shows a gentle and half-playful disappointment in Gawain, for he, the supposed flower of courtesy, is too awkward to ask for a kiss, too tongue-tied to flirt properly, and too cold to take pity on her. Gawain, on the other hand, is caught between two obligations. He must not take from Bercilak's wife anything which he is not willing, according to the terms of his agreement, to hand over to Bercilak, but at the same time he must not lapse from the standards of polite behavior. He can no more solve his problem by sending Bercilak's wife off with a flea in her ear than by sleeping with her; in either case, he would be admitting that it is impossible to reconcile truth and honor with courteous social behavior, and so would be admitting the inadequacy of the civilization which he represents.

While Gawain is at Bercilak's castle the scene alternates steadily between the bedroom, where Gawain and Bercilak's wife parley, and the forest, where Bercilak hunts a variety of animals. There is an explicit parallel drawn between Bercilak and Gawain as a result of their agreement to trade their daily winnings, and a less obvious parallel in that they are both struggling with nature: Bercilak tries, in accordance with the elaborate traditional customs of the hunt, to subdue animals; Gawain tries, in accordance with various formalized and ceremonious patterns of behavior, to fight the temptations of the flesh. But also, of course, Gawain is the hunted, since he is pursued by Bercilak's wife in just the way that the animals are pursued by Bercilak.

The resulting image of Gawain is of a man who thinks that he is a hero, venturing out on a quest, but who is in fact a victim, pursued by enemies whose nature he perceives only dimly. Gawain realizes that the world is dangerous, but the dangers which threaten him the most are never the ones he expects. This is neatly illustrated by the series of tests to which he is subjected. The first test, the challenge to the beheading game, is apparently straightforward enough, but even here Gawain must have had a surprise, unless we suppose that he was a student of folk tales, since there is usually not much to fear from a man who has been beheaded. The second test, the agreement to exchange a day's winnings with Bercilak, seems a pale but exact reflection of the beheading game: in both cases there is an exchange, in both cases Gawain seems to be given the advantage, and in both cases he accepts out of courtesy. But the agreement to exchange winnings seems to Gawain only a Christmas game; he does not recognize it for another, and a more serious, test. During the three days of the exchange, Gawain undergoes what is, in form, a sexual temptation. He realizes this, and so has no trouble in resisting; there is no suggestion that he is ever stirred dangerously by sexual desire. He also succeeds, though sometimes with difficulty, in avoiding the great variety of more concealed traps which are laid for him by Bercilak's wife. He is not provoked into proving his masculinity; he does not get confused about the obligations of courtesy; he does not take the proffered opportunity to escape tactfully by saying that he loves another; he does not accept a valuable ring from Bercilak's wife; and he does not display false generosity by giving a present to her. The final offer of the green girdle seems to come when the test is over, after Bercilak's wife has given up any hope of compromising Gawain. Like the fox Bercilak hunts, Gawain eludes every pursuit until he is suddenly faced with a danger from a totally unexpected direction: although he has resisted so many fleshly temptations, he is finally overcome by the strongest of all natural desires, the wish for self-preservation.

Gawain is closer to Milton's Adam than to Homer's Achilles, for the qualities demanded of him are not the traditional heroic virtues, but the Christian qualities of patience, steadfastness, and faith. The only action required of him is an apparently absurd one: he must seek out his executioner and await a fatal blow. The final scene of the poem, in which Gawain at last receives the blow, serves as an epitome of the entire work. Gawain leaves Bercilak's castle for the rendezvous, is tempted by his guide to abandon the enterprise, but succeeds, after some efforts, in finding the Green Knight. Gawain does flinch from death once, at the Green Knight's first feint, just as he weakened once in accepting the green girdle, but then he recovers and awaits the blow with apparent willingness. There is a strong element of paradox and anticlimax throughout the scene. The formidable and ferocious Green Knight is revealed to be an amiable admirer of Gawain. The decapitating blow turns out to be a mere nick which will serve as healthful penance. The scene itself, so deathlike in its geography and in its season, turns out to be a place of rebirth. But the central paradox is essentially Christian: Gawain has almost lost his life, by seeking to keep it, and has found his life, by being willing to lose it.

At the end of the poem we are given some conflicting opinions. The Green Knight says that Gawain is "On þe fautlest freke þat euer on fote ʒede" ("One of the most faultless men who ever walked"), but Gawain describes himself as "fawty and falce" ("faulty and false"). Gawain wears the green girdle as a badge of his shame; when he relates his story to Arthur's court and shows them the girdle, they laugh loudly and all adopt similar emblems—and he is "honoured þat hit hade euermore after." As a comedy, the poem should lead to self-knowledge, but it does so, for Gawain, only in a limited sense: he recognizes his limitations, but not his success. The real knowledge which the poem leads to is the audience's knowledge of mankind, and here again we are left with paradoxes: we see Gawain as someone bound by his flesh, but able to rise above it; as a glorious, and slightly ridiculous, hero.

PART ONE

Interpretations

The Alliterative Revival

by Dorothy Everett

The Gawain stanza consists of a varying number of alliterative long lines terminated by five short rhyming lines (the 'bob and the wheel'). So far as is known, it is unique though related to other stanza forms which employ the alliterative long line; but, if the poet did not invent it himself, he was fully alive to its potentialities. For the most part he develops his story in the leisurely long lines, using the crisp, rapid lines of the 'bob and wheel' for special purposes, to sum up or conclude a part of the action,[1] for gnomic comments upon it, not unlike some in *Beowulf* (562 ff.), and for remarks that need to be given special force or point (2280). It is noticeable that it is in the last, specially emphatic, line of the 'wheel' that we are told the most surprising fact about the mysterious visitor to Arthur's hall—that he was 'oueral enkergrene.'[2] The poet adapts his long lines to a wide variety of effects; his management of subtle and witty conversation in this seemingly unsuitable medium shows exceptional metrical skill. There is a danger, with a stanza that ends so emphatically, that the narrative might seem to move in a series of jerks, but this effect is minimized by varying the length of the stanzas so that their ends can often be made to coincide with natural pauses, and further counteracted by the device, common in alliterative poetry, of linking the stanzas by repetition. Here this device is unobtrusively used, and in varied forms; an idea, a word, or the alliteration is caught up by the first line of a stanza from some line in the preceding 'wheel.' The repeats are not carried mechanically

---

"The Alliterative Revival" by Dorothy Everett. From *Chapter 3* of Essays on Middle English Literature, *ed. Patricia Kean (Oxford: Clarendon Press, 1955), pp. 74–85. Copyright 1955 by the Clarendon Press. Reprinted by permission of the publisher.
[1] 487 ff., 991 ff.

[2] 'bright green all over.'

right through the poem, but there are enough of them to impart a sense of continuity.

The subtle variations of common practices seen in the meter of *Sir Gawain* are characteristic of the poem in every aspect. It is, of course, immediately recognizable as a romance. Its strange and thrilling story, its setting, the preoccupations of the characters, are all of a kind to satisfy the taste of a reader of romances. It even displays such minor features of the romances as the call for attention, the list of famous knights, the references to the 'book' whence the story came. But the differences between *Sir Gawain* and most Middle English romances are striking. It is no simple tale of adventure and love, but the story of a test of character for which adventure and love-making provide the means. This in itself would give the poem a unity uncommon in romances, but, in addition, the poet concentrates on one adventure of his hero, avoiding the temptation to dwell on others, though he mentions them.

On the other hand, the plot of his chosen episode is complex, combining two stories, known as the Beheading Game and the Temptation, which are found only separately in earlier works. . . . Both stories, it will be observed, present a test—the first of courage and fidelity to the plighted word, the second primarily of chastity, though loyalty to the host and fidelity are involved, and Gawain's courtesy, the quality for which he was famous, is also tested. The combination of the two results, therefore, in a comprehensive test of knightly virtue. There is, in this poem, no mere lip-service to the ideals of chivalry; its purpose is to expound them by illustration, and as it proceeds we become aware that to live up to them requires constant vigilance and self-discipline, and, in the last resort, divine protection. The first concern of the poem is thus with conduct; that is, it is moral in the true sense of the word.

The attitude in the poem towards the art of love is interesting. The lady of the castle thinks (or pretends to think) that Gawain's reluctance to make love to her is unexpected and even unnatural[3] and, in spite of his disclaimers, he does know how to speak the language of love and is not, therefore, quite as ignorant of the art as he tries to make out. But he regards the love which the lady offers and demands as a sin, a temptation to be guarded against.[4] At no point in the poem is there

[3] 1509 ff.
[4] 1549–51, 1774–5.

any trace of the idea, stressed for example in Chaucer's *Troilus and Criseyde* and common among apologists for Courtly Love, that love is an ennobling force, the source of knightly virtues. It is significant of Gawain's attitude, and perhaps of the poet's, that when the lady says she would choose him above all others for her lord, he replies 'Ʒe haf waled wel better';[5] for to recommend a husband as more desirable than a lover is hardly in accordance with the usual canons of Courtly Love. It is also significant that, while there is much talk of love at Bertilak's castle, which is a place of temptation, there is none in Arthur's court, which is not. Clearly, the poet has made his own choice among the qualities customarily held to be proper to a knight, and his choice accords with Christian morality.

Yet, moral as the poem is, the poet rarely moralizes. His conception of the Christian gentleman is conveyed through the actions and speeches of the characters and, in particular, of Gawain. At the same time none of the characters is a mere peg on which to hang a moral, like Chaucer's Griselde. From the first swift sketch of Arthur:

> He watȝ so joly of his joyfnes, and sumquat childgered:
> His lif liked him lyȝt, he louied þe lasse
> Auþer to longe lye or to longe sitte,
> So bisied him his ȝonge blod and his brayn wylde[6]—

we feel ourselves in the presence of living flesh and blood. The preposterous visitor, green (the fairy color) from top to toe and riding a green horse, huge and 'aghlich,' [7] is mysterious enough at first, but he gradually takes shape as the poet minutely describes his appearance, his clothes, his horse and its trappings; and his speech and his movements completely establish him as a living being. It is impossible to doubt his reality when, his challenge uttered, he stands awaiting the blow and:

> Wyth sturne schere þer he stod he stroked his berde,
> And wyth a countenaunce dryȝe he droȝ doun his cote.[8]

[5] 'You have chosen much better' (1276).
[6] 'He was so gay in his youthfulness and somewhat boyish: he liked a merry life and cared the less either to lie long or sit long; so his young blood and wild brain stirred him' (86–9).
[7] 'terrible.'
[8] 'With grim countenance, as he stood there, he stroked his beard, and, with unmoved face, he drew down his coat' (334–5).

But his reality does not make his behavior any the less alarming, and, as he rushes out of the hall, carrying his head in his hand, there is such a sudden relaxation of tension that we are not surprised when Arthur and Gawain find relief in laughter: 'At þat grene[9] þay laʒe and grenne.'

Gawain is, naturally, more fully drawn than any other character. Not only do we observe him ourselves, we are told how he impressed other people in the story and how he himself thought and felt. We see him behaving, as all expect him to do, with exquisite courtesy; but we also see what is not apparent to the other characters, that such behavior does not always come easily to him. All the time that he is parrying the lady's advances, we are aware that he feels himself to be on a knife-edge between discourtesy and compliance:

> For þat pryncece of pris depresed hym so þikke,
> Nurned hym so neʒe þe þred, þat nede hym bihoued
> Oþer lach þer hir luf, oþer lodly refuse.
> He cared for his cortaysye, lest craþayn he were,
> And more for his meschef, ʒif he schulde make synne.[10]

So, too, we see, behind the actions that proclaim his courage, his inward fears and anxieties. Throughout his stay in Bertilak's castle his mind is continually occupied with the perilous meeting at the Green Chapel. He is worried lest he may not arrive in time, and, very naturally, he is fearful about what will happen to him there. He has bad dreams and sleeps little on the night before he is to set out. When he agrees to accept the lady's gift of the green girdle that will preserve his life, and promises to keep it secret, we understand how he came to do so because we have shared the anxiety that brought him to it. But justice would not be done if, at the end, when the Green Knight reveals his knowledge of Gawain's fault, we were still to feel with Gawain and were to concur in the bitter condemnation which he heaps upon himself. So here we are given another and less biased point of view when the Green Knight proclaims him: 'On þe fautlest freke þat euer on fote ʒede';[11] and this judgement is confirmed for us when

---

[9] 'green one,' i.e. the Green Knight (464).

[10] 'For that noble lady (princess) pressed him so hard, urged him so near the limit (thread), that he must needs either accept her love there or rudely refuse. He was anxious for his courtesy, lest he should behave like a villain, and more for his own harm if he were to commit sin . . .' (1770–4).

[11] 'One of the most faultless men that ever walked' (2363).

Arthur's court decrees that the green girdle shall be worn ever after as a sign of honor.

Thus, by the double process of revealing his hero's mind and letting other persons in the story comment upon him, the poet makes us judge his hero's character and conduct as he would have us do. But this alone would not make Gawain the intensely vital figure that we feel him to be. It is what he says and does that gives this impression. The poet has an unusually sharp eye for movements that are natural, or specially significant, at the moment when they are made. 'Now take your grim weapon, and let's see how you deal a blow,' cries the Green Knight to Gawain. 'Gladly, sir,' he replies, and 'his ax he strokes.' On the occasion of the lady's first visit, it is by a series of slight movements that the poet brings the whole scene to life. Gawain is lying in bed:

> And as he slipped in and out of sleep, he heard a little noise, warily, at his door and heard it quickly open. And he lifted up his head out of the bed-clothes and pulled up a corner of the curtain a little and warily looked out to see what it might be. It was the lady, very fair to see, who drew the door after her softly and secretly, and moved towards the bed. And the man was embarrassed and stealthily lay down and behaved as if he were asleep (1182–90).

When he speaks, Gawain's tone varies with the occasion. Naturally courteous in speech, he is exaggeratedly so in his request to Arthur to be allowed to accept the Green Knight's challenge (343), for Arthur's prestige has suffered from the insulting behavior of the Green Knight. In his polite answers to the lady there is something labored, though he can make some neat counterstrokes. There are, too, some subtle indications that with each of her visits, he is a little less on his guard; he addresses her rather more intimately, and once, during the third visit, he slips from the formal plural (ye, you) into the familiar singular:

> I wolde I hade here
> Þe leuest þing for þy luf þat I in londe welde.[12]

As he exchanges jests with Bertilak in the castle he affects a hearty tone; but when he meets him as the Green Knight at the Green Chapel he speaks without ceremony and very much to the point.

The background against which the characters play their parts is

[12] 'I wish I had here the most precious thing I possess on earth, for love of thee' (1801–2).

always concretely presented; and this writer, like other alliterative poets, is lavish with his details. The three hunts, Gawain's armor, the clothes he was given at the castle, and even the cushions placed on his chair—all these, and much more, are minutely described. For the most part, the things the poet chooses to describe are those elaborated by other romance writers; but he had a mind stored with unusually vivid memories of sight and sound; and he knew how to select the telling details and phrases that would convey them. The cold weather is made sensible by the reference to 'mony bryddeӡ vnblyþe[13] . . . Þat pitosly þer piped for pyne of þe colde' (746–7). A brief simile sets before us the whole elaborate structure of Bertilak's castle standing out against the sky: 'pared out of papure[14] purely hit semed' (802). In many of the descriptions there is movement. In the hunting scenes, the ceaseless activity of the hunted animals, of the men and the hounds, conveys all the excitement of the chase. Like Chaucer, the poet can give the impression of a number of people doing different things at the same time, and both in Arthur's hall and in Bertilak's castle, though our chief attention is on the main characters, we are conscious of the bustling life that goes on around them.

In description, as in most else, the poet varies his method of presentation. Sometimes he uses comparison, as in the description of the two ladies in the castle:

> Bot vnlyke on to loke þo ladyes were,
> For if þe ӡonge watӡ ӡep, ӡolӡe watӡ þat oþer;
> Riche red on þat on rayled ayquere,
> Rugh ronkled chekeӡ þat oþer on rolled.[15]

Sometimes, instead of an objective account, he describes things as they appeared to the hero, as in the long account of Bertilak's castle, first seen in the distance, shining and shimmering through the great oaks that surround it. Coming up to it, Gawain finds the draw-bridge up and the gates fast shut. He stops and notices first the deep double moat, the stone walls going down into the water and rising thence a huge height up to the cornices. Then, his eyes having travelled to the top, he sees the watch-towers, and, farther in, the hall

[13] 'unhappy.'
[14] 'cut out of paper.'
[15] 'But unlike in appearance were those ladies; for if the younger was fresh, the other was yellow; a brilliant complexion adorned the one; rough wrinkled cheeks hung in folds on the other' (950–3).

and a mass of towers, pinnacles, chimneys, and roofs. The details are presented in the order in which they would appear to a man arriving at the castle.

Most of the descriptions of nature are related to Gawain in some way or other. Gawain is lying sleepless in bed, thinking of the coming day's meeting with the Green Knight, while

> Þe snawe snitered ful snart, þat snayped þe wylde;
> Þe werbelande wynde wapped fro þe hyȝe,
> And drof vche dale ful of dryftes ful grete';[16]

and the foul weather sharpens his fears, and ours for him. The description of the seasons at the beginning of Part II, conventional enough in some of its details, serves a double purpose. It introduces a fresh section of the story, as similar passages do in the romance of *Kyng Alysaunder* and elsewhere; and, prefaced by the warning,

> A ȝere ȝernes full ȝerne, and ȝeldeȝ neuer lyke,
> Þe forme to þe fynisment foldeȝ ful selden.[17]

it suggests the rapid passing of the year's respite granted to Gawain. It is thus another example of the poet's power of turning to fresh account something that is familiar, as a result of which the familiar does not stale his work, but enriches it by the associations it brings.

To play upon associations of all kinds is natural to this poet, and his magic in large part depends on it, especially in *Pearl*. In *Sir Gawain* it is perhaps chiefly by the words he chooses that he calls up the associations he wants. In the central part of the story, for instance, he alternates between the technical terms of hunting, which would claim the serious attention of those skilled in the sport, and the equally technical terms of love-making. But it is the words belonging to the alliterative tradition that are most effectively used in this poem. When the poet wishes to curdle the blood by indefinable terrors, he chooses ancient words belonging to the vocabulary of alliterative poetry. The Green Knight, he thinks, might be 'half etayn.'[18] The dread creatures which Gawain encountered on his

[16] 'The snow whipped down very sharply, and nipped the wild creatures cruelly, the whistling wind blew from the heights and drove each valley full of great drifts' (2003-5).

[17] 'A year runs full swiftly and never brings back the same thing; the beginning seldom accords with the end' (498-9).

[18] 'giant,' with a strong suggestion of the supernatural; OE. *eoten*. In Beowulf *eotenas* are among the evil brood descended from Cain.

journey (and which the poet does not want to delay over) are swiftly
conveyed by words like 'wormeʒ,' [19] 'wodwos,' [20] and again, 'etayneʒ':

> Sumwhyle wyth wormeʒ he werreʒ, and with wolues als,
> Sumwhyle wyth wodwos þat woned in þe knarreʒ;
> Boþe wyth bulleʒ and bereʒ, and boreʒ oþerquyle,
> And etayneʒ, þat hym anelede of þe heʒe felle.[21]

With all the wealth of detail that is to be found in every part of
the poem, there is never any lack of control. On the contrary, the
poet has succeeded in fashioning a narrative not merely unified but
cunningly and satisfyingly shaped. The fourfold division suggested
by the larger capitals and the flourishes in the manuscript, brings
into relief the essential features of the story: the challenge and Gawain's acceptance of it, his journey and arrival at Bertilak's castle, the
temptation, the second meeting with the Green Knight; but, where
the breaks might be too disrupting, the parts are linked by passages
giving warning of what is to come.

These passages are one of the means by which the poet creates and
maintains a feeling of tension which he heightens and brings to its
climax in Part III. The theme of the Beheading Game is kept in the
reader's consciousness throughout, even when the second theme of the
Temptation occupies the foreground. The skill with which, in the
last two parts, the two are kept running concurrently, each being
brought to the fore at the right moment, can justly be placed to the
credit of the *Gawain* poet, even if, as many believe, he knew a French
poem which combined them. For, unless the English is a mere literal
translation (and it can hardly be this) there are many possibilities of
going astray in so delicate a matter.

Yet there is a good deal more to the ordering of the poem than
this. The poet has produced, as it were, an internal and an external
order at the same time. While the character and actions of the hero
give coherence and meaning to the events of the story, making of
them a unified narrative, the events are also so ordered as to produce

[19] 'dragons,' the *wyrmas* of OE. poetry.
[20] 'wood-trolls,' OE. *wudu-wasa*.
[21] 'Sometimes he fights with dragons, and with wolves too, sometimes with trolls
that dwelt in the crags; both with bulls and bears and at other times with boars,
and with giants that snorted after him from the high fell' (720–3).

something of the effect of a pattern. This 'patterning' is made by the
parallelism of incident or description; it is most obvious, of course, in
the scenes at Bertilak's castle, where it is also most complex. The
parallelism between the three hunts and the three visits of the lady,
and also that between Gawain's blow on New Year's Day and the
Green Knight's on the same day a year later, may have been provided
by the poet's source, though nothing exactly like them is known
elsewhere. But, even so, there are others, less likely to be in any
source. The action of the poem ends as it began, with a scene in Arthur's court, preceded in the one case and followed in the other by a
similarly worded reference to Brutus and the siege of Troy. Gawain's
ordeal is preceded and followed by an adventurous journey, though
because the climax of the story is over, his journey home is much
more lightly sketched. There is some parallel between Gawain's arrival at Bertilak's court, and the festivities that follow, and the festivities at Arthur's court and the arrival of the Green Knight. But this is
an extreme instance of the combination of similarity of theme and
dissimilarity of detail which marks all the parallels; indeed, in some
ways these two descriptions are rather the antithesis of one another,
since, for the defiance and insolence of the Green Knight we have
the courtesy of Sir Gawain, and for the terrified hostility of Arthur's
court, the genial friendliness of Bertilak and his household. This sort
of effect has its nearest analogy in music and can give the same kind
of pleasure as variations on a musical theme. It is undoubtedly an
outcome of rhetorical teaching, but it is rare to find among Middle
English poets one who knows how to make organic use of this teaching.

It is easy to relate most things in this poem to various sources and
influences, it may be that the combination in it of some of the best
things in the alliterative tradition with some of the best in French
romance makes for its richness of texture as compared with most other
Middle English romances. But there is a limit to what can reasonably
be attributed to any outside influence. It was not from literature
that the poet learned the delicacy of touch with which he handles
the scenes between Gawain and the lady, or the understanding of
human feeling shown in the blustering words of Gawain as he hears
the Green Knight whetting his axe behind the rock. Gawain has not
yet seen him and is not sure precisely what the noise is, and he speaks
half fearfully, half ironically:

'Bi Godde,' quoþ Gawayn, 'þat gere, as I trowe,
Is ryched at þe reuerence me, renk, to mete
    bi rote.' 22

Such things are not to be explained, they can only be remarked and enjoyed; and this poem is fuller of them than any contemporary work save that of Chaucer.

A comparison with Chaucer is not, indeed, wholly to the disadvantage of the lesser-known poet, for he surpasses Chaucer in some things—in architectonics, for instance, and perhaps in natural description—and, though his range is narrow, within it he shows himself a subtle delineator of character. In outlook he is as civilized as Chaucer, but sterner, much more of a moralist, a great deal less of a humorist. But there is humor of a sort in his presentation of the Green Knight's play-acting in Arthur's hall, and in some of Gawain's rueful remarks; and the poet has some of Chaucer's capacity for seeing his story and his characters from both inside and out, so that his readers can sympathize with the hero and at the same time see him and his doings in perspective.

²² 'By God,' said Gawain, 'that contraption, I believe, is meant for a salutation, to meet me, by the way' (2205-7).

Art and Tradition
in *Sir Gawain and the Green Knight*

by *Larry D. Benson*

Variation: The Narrative Structure

The major importance of variation to the critic of *Sir Gawain* is the key it provides to the structure and meaning of the narrative, for the style of this poem is organic, and its basic stylistic trait affects every part of the work. The structure of the sentence, with its varied parallel constructions, its ellipses, its dependence on juxtaposition and analysis, is the model for the narrative as a whole. Because the style of the individual line and sentence has been so imperfectly understood, the structure and meaning of the poem have never been clear. It is no accident that the "unity" of the best alliterative poems has been a central problem for their critics, for the reader who approaches them with the same concept of structure that he brings to Chaucer or Gower is apt to find them badly constructed and poorly unified—a judgment that has been passed at some time or other on every good alliterative poem from *Beowulf* to *Sir Gawain*. Scenes and episodes in such works do not exist in the straightforward causal order of most narratives. Each forms part of a series of variations composed of other passages similar in form and content, and the meaning of each is modified and illuminated by its variations, even though, as in the sentence, their relation is implied rather than stated explicitly.

The Chaucerian style leads to a completely different kind of narra-tive. Chaucer designates his characters with a small, repetitive vocabu-

From **Art and Tradition in Sir Gawain and the Green Knight** *by Larry D. Ben-son* (*New Brunswick, N. J.: Rutgers University Press, 1965*), *pp. 158–64, 240–48. The original footnotes have been omitted, and translations have been supplied. Copy-right © 1965 by Rutgers, The State University. Reprinted by permission of the publisher.*

lary. He elaborately insists upon the exact designation, and his apparent eagerness to avoid ambiguity even leads him to combine the demonstrative adjective with the proper noun—"Lo heere this Arcite and this Palamoun." That construction never appears in the work of the Gawain-poet; he often designates his character by "the" plus a noun—"þe knyʒt"—a construction that Chaucer almost never uses. Chaucer's syntax is marked by the same insistence on clear and exact specification—"Bifil that in that seson on a day"—and his narrative technique as a whole is characterized by the same trait. In *The Knight's Tale*, for example, when the narrator shifts from one line of action to another, he emphatically signals the transition to his audience:

> Now wol I stynte of Palamon a lite,
> And lete hym in his prisoun stille dwelle,
> And of Arcita forth I wol yow telle.
>
> (*KT*, 1334–36)

When the Gawain-poet shifts from one line of action to another, he does so within a single sentence:

> Þe lede with þe ladyeʒ layked alle day,
> Bot þe lorde ouer þe londeʒ launced ful ofte,
> Sweʒ his vncely swyn . . .
>
> (vv. 1560–62)

[The man with the ladies sported all day, but the lord dashed often over the countryside, pursues his ferocious boar . . .]

> And ʒe he lad hem bi lagmon, þe lorde and his meyny,
> On þis maner bi þe mountes quyle myd-ouer-under,
> Whyle þe hende knyʒt at home holsumly slepes,
> Withinne þe comly cortynes . . .
>
> (vv. 1729–32)

[And indeed he led them by devious ways, the lord and his company, in this manner by the hills until midday, while the courteous knight at home sleeps healthfully, within the fair bed-hangings . . .]

Chaucer avoids such abrupt transitions because as a narrator he is so eager to confide in us; he does not want us to miss his meaning. His *Knight's Tale* is built on parallels and contrasts as finely wrought as those in *Sir Gawain*, but he is not content to leave his tale without Theseus' explicit pointing of the moral. In the *Troilus* Chaucer himself draws the meaning out for us, standing apart from his story to address the "yonge fresshe folkes, he or she." In the Gawain-poet's narrative, as within the sentence, the variations are juxtaposed without comment and the meaning is allowed to emerge from the structure. Gawain and the Green Knight each have a last word, and the less personal voice of the narrator does not intrude to tell us which is right.

H. L. Savage's analysis of the relation between the hunting and temptation scenes is probably the best-known explanation of narrative variation in *Sir Gawain* (though Savage, of course, does not call it "variation"). Until his article appeared few critics understood the structure of the poem; indeed, one scholar argued for an English source on the basis of the apparent lack of skill with which the parts are joined together. The two sets of scenes that Savage studied seem completely different. One takes place in a bedroom, the other in the forest. One concerns the niceties of courtship, the other the vigorous excitement of the chase, and one is almost pure action, the other almost pure dialogue. Yet, much as these two sets of scenes differ in content and emphasis, their form is the same. As Savage demonstrates, they are almost exactly parallel, providing different but parallel viewpoints on a situation whose meaning can be understood only in the light of both narratives. Taken alone, Bercilak's hunt is just an exciting account of the chase, the temptation scenes sophisticated bedroom comedy with a ludicrous reversal of roles. Together they are a set of variations that blend to point up the nature of Gawain's trial and the extent of Bercilak's involvement in it. The lady, we realize, is not merely attempting to enjoy her lord's absence. She is as intent upon her prey as Bercilak upon his. Bercilak's pursuit of his quarry becomes a commentary on the lady's pursuit of Gawain, and Gawain's skillful replies become meaningful as the desperate fox "trantes and tornayeeȝ" in parallel fashion, finally attempting to escape through trickery only to run upon Bercilak's waiting sword.

The parallel series of scenes themselves have other parallel variations throughout the poem; Bercilak's capture of the fox is related to his final capture of Gawain, and its form is related to each of the previous hunts and to the lady's final victory. The lady's scene of triumph is related both to the hunts and previous temptations and to the other scenes in which bargains are made and broken, from the challenge itself, to the guide's temptation of the hero, to the final confrontation between Gawain and the Green Knight. The same principles that Savage discovered in the temptation scenes appear wherever one looks in the poem, for the parallel juxtaposition of apparently unrelated episodes is the basic characteristic of the narrative, appearing even in the combination of the parallel but contrasting temptation and beheading tales, which posed the major problem of unity for the early critics.

Within the narrative one also finds the same sort of periodic, bracketing frameworks that contain and control the variations within the sentence. In the first fit, for example, each major stage of the action has its parallel variation, and each set of variations is bracketed within a limiting framework. The scene opens and closes with the feast that brackets the episode, which is indeed, as Arthur tells Guenevere, an "interlude" occurring between its courses. Within that framework is the Green Knight's amazing entrance and equally astonishing departure. When he enters, the action of his entry is suspended for the description of him and his equipment, which, as we have seen, is actually two descriptions juxtaposed by means of variation. Then the entry resumes and, once in the hall, the Green Knight states his challenge; the conditions he states are repeated, with more sinister overtones, when he leaves. Then Arthur accepts the challenge, but Gawain interrupts the action as suddenly as the Green Knight had done, and he also makes a request of Arthur. The king grants his request, and he kneels to receive the axe, just as the Green Knight, after a restatement of the bargain, bows to receive Gawain's blow, which is, of course, parallel to the blow that Arthur begins to deliver. The beheading is the heart of the episode, surrounded by the parallel structures. And the whole episode, including the feast itself, is enclosed within yet another set of parallel passages, the catalogue of Arthur's ancestors and the narrator's characterization of the king at the beginning of the poem, followed by his new comments on the king at the end of the first fit and the catalogue of the seasons at the beginning of the next.

In its broad outlines the entire poem is constructed on the same principle. It begins with the Troy story and a scene of happy celebration. Then follow the challenge and the beheading, the arming and departure of Gawain, and his journey to Bercilak's castle. There, after more banqueting, he undergoes three days of temptation, each day parallel to the others and all three days paralleled by the hunting scenes. Then Gawain again arms and departs. There is another journey, the return-blow, and finally the journey back to Camelot, where there is yet another celebration at court and a final reference to the Troy legend at the poem's end. The beheading plot brackets the temptation within its parallel delivery and return-blows, and the temptation itself is composed on a complex of variations within that framework.

From the standpoint of Chaucerian verse, this seems a peculiar and subtle method of narration. However, it was common in the poet's own literary tradition. The best Old English poetry was also built on the principle of structural variation. Poems like *The Wanderer* and *Seafarer* depend for their effect on parallel, secular and religious, restatements of the speakers' situations, and *Beowulf,* like *Sir Gawain,* is concentrated on a relatively small number of episodes that resemble one another in structure and content (Beowulf's three battles with the monsters) and that form significant parallel contrasts (Beowulf's initial triumph and final tragic death). The structure of the narrative is concentrated and appositional, enclosed within the framework of the burials at the beginning and end. Evidently some of the Old English narrative techniques survived even in Middle English alliterative poetry, since one finds the same concern with parallels, contrasts, and variations in the narrative structure of poems such as *Morte Arthure, Golagros and Gawane,* and the *Awntyrs of Arthur* (all, like *Sir Gawain,* Arthurian poems of the northern, heavily ornamented and formulaic tradition of alliterative verse).

So ancient a technique could be used in the fourteenth century, because the general aesthetic of the period was especially favorable to this kind of structural variation; the juxtaposition of parallel, opposing elements without an explicit statement of their relation is basically the technique of "dramatic conflict" that, as Hauser writes, dominates "the whole relation of Gothic art to nature and the inner structure of its composition." When the contrast is between the courtly and the churlish or the sacred and the profane—between such completely contrasting characters as Gawain and the Green Knight—the dramatic conflict is late Gothic *par excellence.* We more decorous moderns are sometimes apt to overlook this principle, considering (as museums and photographs sometimes force us to do) only the marvellous statue of the Virgin and overlooking the equally marvellous grotesquerie that exists alongside it, reading the *Inferno* without the *Paradiso* or the tales of the Miller and Reeve without those of the Knight and Man of Law.

*   *   *

The Return to Camelot

The most trying of all Gawain's humiliations at the Green Chapel
is the fact that the Green Knight refuses to take him seriously. When
Gawain, finally brought to true repentance, offers reparation, "Thenn
loȝe þat oþer leude" (v. 2389). It is not the harsh laughter of the moralist but the tolerant laughter of one who recognizes the comedy of the
situation. Gawain must be his own moralist, solemnly invoking the
fall of Adam and Samson without realizing the absurdity of scaling
his bedroom adventure against their cosmic tragedies. Worse yet, from
Gawain's point of view, is the reaction of his fellow knights. When
he returns to tell his sad tale in Camelot, he groans for grief and
blushes for shame. But Arthur's courtiers only "Laȝen loude þerat" (v.
2514.)

Gawain does not join in the laughter. He remains, in aspiration at
least, the chevalier, and he judges his actions from the standpoint of
that demanding ideal. Much as he has learned, his character has not
been greatly altered. It is not possible for the poet to allow so drastic
a change as Gawain would have to undergo to accomplish this. As the
laughter of the Green Knight and the court shows, what Gawain really
learns from his adventure is that chivalry takes itself a bit too seriously,
that men become ridiculous and foolish when they attempt to live up
to so superhuman an ideal. Yet it would be a failure of tact for Gawain to make light of his own actions, and it would be almost impossible for him to do this without rejecting chivalry itself, and that is not
the poet's purpose. Therefore, Gawain remains a knight, unable to
judge himself with the uncourtly tolerance of Bercilak.

The court to which he returns can and does change, and it is
amused rather than discomfited by the adventure. Gawain was its representative in the adventure, and now it becomes his surrogate in the
last stanzas of the poem. It can make light of Gawain's actions without
rejecting chivalry, for it is possible for the court to laugh at him and
yet receive him back into its membership. The laughter is good-
humored, for in laughing at Gawain, their representative, they are
laughing at themselves. They accept him with both his one fault and
his knighthood into the court, and they decide that in the future he
will not be alone in wearing his badge of "blame." They agree that,

> Vche burne of þe broþerhede, a bauderyk schulde haue,
> A bende abelef hym aboute of a bryȝt grene,

And þat, for sake of þat segge, in swete to were.
For þat watȝ acorded þe renoun of þe Rounde Table,
And he honoured þat hit hade euermore after.

(vv. 2516-20)

[Each man of the brotherhood should have a baldric, a bend slantwise about him of a bright green, and, following suit, wear it for sake of that man. For that token was accorded to be the glory of the Round Table, and he was honored that had it, evermore after.]

The renown survives. The touch of villainy did not, as Gawain feared, destroy the virtues "þat longeȝ to knyȝteȝ" (v. 2381), but, as the laughter shows, the fame of the Round Table and the ideal it represents is now modified by the bend of bright green and the tolerant acknowledgment of human limitations that it implies.

This is not the way a romance is supposed to end; the glorious affirmation of the hero's virtues and of the ideal he represents is conspicuously absent. Yet *Sir Gawain* could hardly end in any other way, for this final scene is only an extension of the recurrent alternation of romance and unromantic elements that repeatedly undercuts the high seriousness of the narrative. The poet never allows us to view Gawain's actions in the simple light of romance, and Gawain's heroic deeds and attitudes are constantly juxtaposed with the comic or humiliating. With a grand disregard of consequences and a high romantic sense of duty he rises to accept the challenge; but then, instead of applauding him as a romance narrator should, the poet intrudes with the common-sense, unidealized observation that "Men ben mery in mynde quen þay han mayn drynk." With heroic resolve Gawain departs from the weeping court only to discover that his shining armor is no protection against the wind and the rain and then to be plunged into the comic frustrations he meets at Bercilak's castle. When he does fulfill the bargain and leaps back to give battle to his antagonist, the Green Knight merely laughs and reveals his knowledge of Gawain's encounter with the lady. Gawain, in a reversal of the pattern of romances like *Caradoc* and *Perceval,* starts as a perfect knight and moves downward, ending where the heroes of those romances began, as an imperfect "fol chevalier" who is the object of laughter rather than admiration. From the standpoint of romance, the poem has been a tragedy, and Gawain bitterly laments his fall from his initial perfection into wretchedness. From Bercilak's unromantic viewpoint Gawain has moved upward and the poem has a comic conclusion; the

hero began, or so he told the challenger, as the least of knights, and he
ends, or so Bercilak tells him, as the best of all.

The Green Knight's judgment on the action must be taken as seriously as Gawain's, for the poet's successful characterization raises him
above the status of a merely negative, anti-romantic character. He has
an attitude of his own, unromantic rather than anti-romantic in its
refusal to take romance seriously. That this attitude is valid and respectable is shown by the narrator's echo of the Green Knight's words
after the first beheading and the court's echo of his laughter after the
second. The tension between romantic and unromantic elements
thus extends even to the possible judgments that the reader can make
on the action. He cannot reject Gawain and what he stands for, for
the romance ideal is noble, reinforced with the powers of religion and
tradition; yet he cannot completely accept it either, for that ideal is
slightly absurd, a bit too narrow, and clearly too demanding for a man
in this world. The poem is thus both a tragic romance with the sad
moral that perfection is beyond our grasp and an unromantic comedy
with the happy point that if a man aims high enough he can come as
near perfection as this world allows.

Such an ambivalent attitude toward the romance ideal reflects
both the underlying seriousness of the Gawain-poet's purposes and
his relation to his own time, for the limitations of the ideal were a
peculiarly fourteenth-century concern. The genre of romance was still
widespread at this time, as it was to remain for another century. Moreover, in theory at least, the romance ideal still offered a code for the
conduct of life, and as yet no Castiglione had provided a secular alter-
native to it. In Edward the Black Prince the previous generation
seemed to have had a living embodiment of that code, one whose example, according to the Chandos Herald, could teach all "to take the
remembrance of good into their hearts and to achieve honor" ("Pour
prendre en lour coers remembrance/ De bien et honour recevoir," vv.
6–7). Yet by the last quarter of the century biographies like the
Chandos Herald's *Life of the Black Prince,* romances like *Sir Degrevant,* and even Gawain's ideals seem already "consciously old-fashioned." This is because, as J. D. Bruce wrote, the ideals of romance
were no longer in accord with "the spirit of contemporary society":

> Perhaps this may account in part, at least, for the fact that the Middle
> English romances, on the whole, are inferior to German productions in
> the same *genre;* for the latter, it will be recalled, fell at the end of the

twelfth century and beginning of the thirteenth—that is to say, it was coincident with all but the first period of production in France itself, and so was a vivid representation of actual contemporary ideals.

Most Middle English romances are indeed inferior for this reason, but the best of them, most notably *Sir Gawain,* are also vivid representations of contemporary attitudes, for they show the scrutiny that older values were undergoing as the Middle Ages came to an end.

The sophisticated man of the fourteenth century had only to look about him to see that the romance ideal no longer fit the life he knew. The "crusades" of this century have nothing but the name in common with the great enterprises of the High Middle Ages, and the few examples of chivalric conduct that Froissart admiringly cites are glaring exceptions in his chronicles of a cruel and greedy era. In England, France, and the Low Countries the peasants were asserting themselves in a way that showed clearly that the old feudal order was dying, while the Great Schism and the rise of heresy showed that even the church was not as secure as it once seemed, and plague and famine threatened the existence of society itself, while those who wished to revive the good old days busied themselves with founding ceremonial orders of knighthood that only preserved in an overelaborate fashion the forms of a previous, mainly fictional age. Perhaps such efforts only intensified the disillusionment, especially in England, where Edward III had so closely identified himself with the Arthurian ideal and where, at the end of the fourteenth century, so many of Edward's projects, most obviously the war with France, were yielding such poor results. The old knightly code retained its glamour, and it still seemed admirable that Edward had solemnly proclaimed the restoration of the Round Table and even that, as *Les Voeux de héron* has it, he began the Hundred Years' War to fulfill a chivalric vow made on the carcass of a heron at a great feast, but the results to which such a devotion to chivalry could lead were there for all to see, and none but the most conservative could ignore the disparity between aspiration and fulfillment or overlook the faults of the ideal itself.

This new, more critical attitude toward romantic chivalry is not restricted to England; it is apparent throughout the art and literature of the later medieval period. In the plastic arts it is reflected not only in the general growth of "bourgeois realism" but also in the handling of specific themes; Bernheimer found that in the combat between the wild man and the knight that so frequently appears in medieval art,

As long as the knightly ideal remained untarnished, the victory in this battle was invariably accorded the knight. It marks a major turning point in the history of European civilization that . . . the wild man is sometimes allowed to win in works of art describing the combat after the middle of the fourteenth century.

In romance the new attitude is evident in the greater emphasis on religious virtues at the expense of chivalry, beginning with the Benedictine and Cistercian prose romancers of the thirteenth century, and in the new interest in the fall of the Round Table and the death of Arthur, which become popular subjects in fourteenth-century romance, in which Arthur himself is used as a tragic *exemplum* of the workings of fortune. In the major Northern English romances of the later fourteenth and fifteenth centuries the Arthurian court and its code are invariably subjected to moral criticism: the stanzaic *Le Morte Arthur* is a tragedy caused by courtly love and broken allegiance; the alliterative *Morte Arthure* is a tragedy of Arthur's ambition, his "surquidré"; the *Awntyrs of Arthur* contains a long attack on the luxury and vainglory of the Round Table; *Golagros and Gawain* presents a completely debased characterization of Arthur; and *Lancelot of the Laik* seems to have been written mainly for the sake of Amyntas' condemnation of the king for pursuing pleasure rather than the good of his people. Though the existence of these works shows how attractive the romance ideal remained, their unanimous criticism shows that its day of dominance had passed. Significantly, Chaucer's model knight is a man well along toward middle age, old enough to have a twenty-year-old son who shows little promise of becoming the Christian knight his father is. Tournaments and courtly love come off rather badly in *Troilus* and *The Knight's Tale,* and Chaucer's only two "English romances" are *The Wife of Bath's Tale,* in which Arthur's knights are mainly noted for rape, and *Sir Thopas.*

The beauty of *Sir Gawain* is that it takes the old ideals neither too lightly nor too seriously. It has comedy, but none of the burlesque of *Sir Thopas*; it condemns knighthood, but lightly and without the heavy-handed morality that impairs the effect of most of the romances listed above. Their authors also admired the knightly ideal despite their recognition of its faults, and their works are also characterized by the tension between condemnation and admiration that we find in *Sir Gawain*. But the Gawain-poet was able to state with delicacy what most of them could say but crudely. His representative of unromantic vitality can finally praise knighthood for what it is because he has no romantic notions of what it should be, and he therefore does not denounce what he finds and call for a return to an unattainable older order, as do Langland and Gower. Gawain, the representative of knighthood, must denounce himself, and in doing so he shows us its most attractive quality, its nobility of aspiration. The noble desire for perfection remains, and Gawain returns to the court and a life of adventure rather than to the hermitage where Arthur's knights end their days in *Le Morte Arthur*. For Gawain to condemn himself and the Green Knight to praise him is a final reversal of expectation; it is the unromantic figure who is supposed to denounce the knight for his pride—the Brahmin in *Alexander and Dindimus*, the "philosophers" in the alliterative *Morte Arthure*, the ghost in the *Awntyrs of Arthur*. This final reversal of roles, part of the exchange we see in the return-blow, is one of the last and most significant variations in the poem, and it is in the variation, in both contrasting speeches, that the meaning lies, for the attitudes they express, indulgent forgiveness and uncompromising aspiration, are both finally maintained by the poem.

In these parallel but contrasting attitudes toward what has happened we can finally see the meaning that was expressed throughout the poem in the most important variation of all, the carefully drawn parallel contrast between the Green Knight and Gawain. When they momentarily exchange roles, the Green Knight becoming temporarily a gentleman and Gawain an unromantic churl, filled with energy, angry speech, and anti-romantic ideas about women, and when they finally part, Gawain to the court and the undefeated Green Knight whithersoever he would, we recognize that the main characters are themselves variations, two parts of the unstated whole that is life itself. Neither can triumph in their conflict because Gawain's ceremonial idealism and the Green Knight's laughing realism are both essential to the better life that the court with its bend of green— ceremonialized and used in a courtly, heraldic fashion—and its good-natured laughter represents at the end of the poem.

The laughter with which the action concludes is exactly the right note, for whatever deeper concerns it has touched and however serious it almost becomes, *Sir Gawain* is predominantly a festive poem. In that spirit it weighs and gently criticizes the ideal of literature and life that was romance, and it suggests that this noble ideal can survive only if it takes account of the rest of life and of the human limitations of even its best representatives. That the poem still has meaning for the reader today is because, though the vocabulary has changed, the conflict between ideal codes and human limitations still persists. That it evidently appeals even more to readers of the twentieth century than to those of the nineteenth may be because our age, in which absolute ideals derived from theory or literature have again become important forces in life, can more easily recognize the value of a poem in which the juxtaposition of churlishness and knighthood, of humility and laughter, of terror and comedy, yields a finely tolerant, vigorously good-natured, and characteristically Gothic acceptance of life both as it is and as it should be. English literature may offer a few, very few better narratives than *Sir Gawain and the Green Knight,* but none more delightful and humane.

The Third Fitt

by J. A. Burrow

The third day, New Year's Eve, is the last of Gawain's stay at the castle; but even if this were not so, the reader might suspect that it would prove critical. Things go by threes at Hautdesert; [1] and anyway the 'third time' traditionally has something special about it—as in Bercilak's proverbial 'þrid tyme þrowe best.' The poet fosters these suspicions, signalling unobtrusively to the reader from time to time as he deals with the first phase of the day's action, the fox-hunt. This starts in a perfectly ordinary way, with the host hearing Mass, eating a 'morsel,' and setting out with men and dogs; but the account of these preparations is accompanied for the first time with a short but vivid description of the weather:

> Ferly fayre watz þe folde, for þe forst clenged;
> In rede rudede vpon rak rises þe sunne,
> And ful clere costez þe clowdes of þe welkyn.
>
> (1694–6)

[1] All threes in the poem are connected with Hautdesert. There are none in the first fitt. The number first occurs in l. 763, where Gawain crosses himself three times and immediately sees the castle. There are three 'motes' on the first day of hunting and testing (1141); three cockcrows (1412) and three dead hounds (1443) on the second; three hounds catching the fox (1713), as well as three kisses, on the third. Notice that the poet—generally careful about times and dates—seems to treat the seven full days of Gawain's stay at Hautdesert (Christmas Day to New Year's Eve, inclusive) as two groups of three days: on the evening of St. John's Day (Dec. 27, the third day of the Christmas feast, see ll. 1020–3), Gawain says he has only 'bare þre dayez' before Jan. 1. What has happened to Dec. 28? Gollancz thinks a line is missing after 1022 (note to 1020–3). See M. R. Watson, 'The Chronology of SGGK', M.L.N., LXIV (1949), pp. 85–6.

[Exceedingly fair was the land, for the frost clung to it; in red, fiery upon
the drifting clouds, rises the sun, and very brightly it coasts by the clouds
of the heavens.]

Here, as when the poet 'tarries' to describe the lady's dress and appearance at the beginning of the following temptation scene, again
for the first time at such a point, the reason for the new amplification
lies in its timing—held back until the beginning of the critical day,
and producing, when it comes, expectancy, a sense of occasion.

Much the most important peculiarity of the third hunting scene,
however, is its quarry, the fox. A lord hunting a fox is a familiar figure
to modern readers—more so, indeed, than a lord hunting deer or boar;
but the evidence clearly suggests that Bercilak's fox-hunt must have
come as a surprise to the poem's contemporary audience. Deer and
boar were considered 'noble game' and, as such, figure quite frequently
in courtly romance, both French and English; but foxes were considered
'vermin,' and fox-hunts are very rare indeed in the romances—if indeed
there are any at all.[2] It must, therefore, have seemed odd that the
author, after two conventional noble hunts, should resort to a 'foul
fox' for his third and final quarry:

> Hunteres vnhardeled bi a holt syde,
> Rocheres roungen bi rys for rurde of her hornes;
> Summe fel in þe fute þer þe fox bade. . . .

                                                                    (1697–9)

[Hunters unleashed hounds by the side of a wood, rocks resounded among
the bushes for the noise of their horns; some hit on the track where the
fox waited . . .]

'*The* fox' is worth noticing. There is nothing, so far as I can see, in the
previous lines to suggest that Bercilak was out to find a fox; yet the
fox is introduced (unlike the boar, ll. 1437–40) as if he were inevitable.
This makes him particularly provoking. Why should it have to be a
fox, of all animals? The reader has only to ask this question—in retrospect, at least—to see the answer. We learn from the poem itself, without resort to medieval animal lore, that the fox is a thief (1725), wily
(1728 and 1905) and a shrew (1896); and we know that on the day of
the fox-hunt Gawain cunningly and wrongfully keeps possession of
what is Bercilak's by right—the girdle. The 'parallel' (though that is
not a good word to describe the actual effect) is obvious—and that

---

[2] See H. L. Savage, *The 'Gawain'-Poet*, pp. 33–5.

whether or not one sees similar parallels on the previous days. Indeed, it seems best to judge the cases separately. I myself cannot see that the second temptation scene differs from the first as the boar-hunt differs from the deer-hunt; but, where the fox-hunt and third temptation are concerned, I see that each differs from both its predecessors in the same sort of way.[3] Each involves a departure from the noble and exemplary conduct of the previous days. In each we recognize death as a terrifying thing which men and animals alike try to escape by every device in their power, regardless of dignity or duty.

The terror and the 'wiles' of the fox are vividly evoked in the first phase of the hunt: the fox dodging and 'tourneying' through the wood, doubling back, stopping to listen, jumping over a hedge to escape into the open, meeting the hounds and swerving back into the wood, making for the open once more and 'reeling in again:'

> And ȝe he lad hem bi lagmon, þe lorde and his meyny,
> On þis maner bi þe mountes quyle myd-ouer-vnder.

(1729–30)

[And indeed he led them by devious ways, the lord and his company, in this manner by the hills until midday.]

Against this background of pursuit and desperate flight, the opening of the ensuing temptation scene takes on a special poignancy and depth. Gawain is not, as before, sleeping soundly. He is restless and mutters in his sleep:

> In dreȝ droupyng of dreme draueled þat noble,
> As mon þat watȝ in mornyng of mony þro þoȝtes,
> How þat destiné schulde þat day dele hym his wyrde
> At þe grene chapel, when he þe gome metes,
> And bihoues his buffet abide withoute debate more.[4]

(1750–4)

[In heavy gloom of dreaming muttered that noble, like one who was sorrowing for many oppressive thoughts, how destiny should that day deal him his fate at the green chapel, when he meets the man, and must abide his blow without further argument.]

---

[3] Savage, op. cit., pp. 35–37. Savage argues his distinction between a deer-like first temptation and a boar-like second on pp. 40–46.

[4] Dante ascribes special powers of prophecy to dawn dreams in *Purgatorio*, IX, ll. 13–18; and Chauntecleer's warning dream comes 'in a dawenynge.' See *S.P.*, XLV (1948), pp. 50–59.

Gawain, like the fox, is afraid; and their common fear of death creates
a context in which the figure of the lady, with her merry mantle,
jewelled hair-net, naked throat and bare breast, assumes something of
a symbolic value. She is like Dame Life, in the alliterative *Death and
Life*:

> Of her druryes to deeme to dull be my witts;
> And the price of her perrye can no person tell;
> And the colour of her kirtle was caruen ffull lowe,
> Þat her blisfull breastes bearnes might behold;
> With a naked necke she neighed ther-till,
> Þat gaue light on the land as leames of the sunn.[5]

[My wits are too dull to estimate her treasures, and no person can tell
the price of her jewelry, and the collar of her gown was cut very low,
that men might behold her blissful breasts; she approached that place
with an uncovered neck that gave light on the land like rays of the sun.]

By her behavior, too, Bercilak's lady represents life's cause—rather as
Boethius' visitor, under similar circumstances, represents that of phi-
losophy. She throws open a window, wakes Gawain from his night-
mares with praise of the morning ('A! mon, how may þou slepe, / Þis
morning is so clere?'), laughs, and kisses him. The 'wallande joye'
which this inspires in the hero is as much *joie de vivre* as anything else;
and the 'blis and bonchef' which follows is in the spirit of Bercilak's
words on the previous evening:

> Make we mery quyl we may and mynne vpon joye,
> For þe lur may mon lach when-so mon lykeȝ.

(1681–2)

[Let us make merry while we may, and think upon joy, for one may
seize sorrow whenever one likes.]

At this point the poet is stacking the cards more than ever against
his hero; and he makes it clear that Gawain is near to losing the game:
'Gret perile bitwene hem stod.' The crisis is not in fact a very real one
for the reader, because the poet contents himself with a summary
description; but the summary is important in itself, because it gives
us, quite explicitly, the poet's understanding of the moral issues at
stake between Gawain and the lady:

[5] Ed. I. Gollancz (Oxford, 1930), ll. 87–92.

For þat pryncece of pris depresed hym so þikke,
Nurned hym so neӡe þe þred, þat nede hym bihoued
Oþer lach þer hir luf, oþer lodly refuse.
He cared for his cortaysye, lest craþayn he were,
And more for his meschef, ӡif he schulde make synne
And be traytor to þat tolke þat þat telde aӡt.

(1770-5)

[For that excellent princess urged him so continuously, pressed him so near to the limit, that of necessity he must either take there her love, or offensively refuse it. He was concerned about his courtesy, lest he be a boor, and more about his evil plight, if he should do sin and be a traitor to the man that owned that dwelling.]

The meaning of this passage is quite clear, up to the last two lines. Gawain is faced with a choice of two evils. If he goes on refusing the lady's love, he must offend her (*'lodly* refuse'); and this would be a real evil, for Gawain *does* 'care for his courtesy.' He cares still more, however, for the 'mischief' he would incur were he to 'lach þer hir luf'—for by so doing he would, the poet says, 'make synne / And be traytor to þat tolke þat þat telde aӡt.' There are two ways of taking these words. Either the line 'And be traytor . . .' specifies the 'synne' (as if it were 'commit sin by being traitor . . .'), or it does not. I think that it does, and that the other reading involves two particularly mischievous errors: first, that the author was so preoccupied with chastity that he could use the word 'sin', without further ado, to mean 'sexual sin' or sin in the Sunday papers' sense; and second, that he did not regard treachery to the host as a sin, properly speaking, at all—or at least that he regarded it as 'taking second place.' [6] On such a view, the serious moral business of the poem is done once the hero has survived his so-called 'chastity test (i.e. after l. 1800 or thereabouts); and his concealing the girdle is no more than a venial fault—a 'breach of the chivalric code', perhaps, but not 'synne'. I shall return to this point later.

After the poet's summary, there follows a short bit of dialogue (ll. 1779-95) in which the lady makes her last attempt to persuade Gawain to accept her love. Her appeal, by comparison with the earlier scenes,

[6] Introduction to Gollancz's edition, p. xxi, n. 1: 'Professor Hulbert . . . says that the test is for loyalty, not chastity. But ll. 1773-5 show that Gawain's chief fear is that he may sin against God, and his duty of loyalty to his host takes second place.' I agree with Professor Hulbert.

is brief, simple, rather lyrical in tone, drawing on the literary traditions
of the slighted maiden's complaint: 'I love you' ('Bifore alle þe wyȝeȝ
in þe worlde wounded in hert') 'and you should love me in return—
unless you already love another.' This elicits from Gawain his last,
and decisive, refusal:

> Þe knyȝt sayde, 'Be sayn Jon,'
> And smeþely con he smyle,
> 'In fayth I welde riȝt non,
> Ne non wil welde þe quile.'

$$(1788-91)$$

[The knight said, "By Saint John," and pleasantly did he smile, "In
faith I possess no one at all, nor do I wish to possess anyone at present."]

The movement of the short lines makes this sound abrupt; but Gawain
is obviously still trying to avoid refusing 'lodly.' The reference to St.
John, if it means anything, means that Gawain is trying to live the
life of celibacy for which that saint was famous[7]—a convenient polite
fiction which harmonizes well with the suggestion of 'In fayth I welde
riȝt non.' The claim in the following line, however, is less grand: 'Ne
non wil welde þe quile.' This would be rude if there were not some
specific and recognizable reason why Gawain should not want a mistress *for the time being*. The reason is, presumably, that he is on a
quest—a reason which he later adduces for not receiving love-tokens
(ll. 1836–8). There are good grounds, part pious, part superstitious,
for a knight to be abstinent while on a quest.[8] The lady, therefore,
has to accept Gawain's declaration at its face value; and this she does,
with a faintly literary grace:

> 'Bot I am swared for soþe, þat sore me þinkkeȝ.
> Kysse me now comly, and I schal cach heþen,

---

[7] Oaths by St. John sometimes seem to have this kind of significance. In the *Earl
of Toulouse* a lady protests her innocence with the words, 'Be Seynte Iohn, / Hore
was y neuyr none' (in French and Hale, *Middle English Metrical Romances*, ll.
793–4). See also *Canterbury Tales* III, 164–8. Both the other two saint-oaths in the
poem have significance. The porter swears by Peter, the porter of heaven (l. 813);
and Bercilak swears by Giles, the friend of a hind (l. 1644).

[8] . . . The mixture of piety and superstition comes out well in the words of
Malory's Lancelot: 'And as for to sey to take my pleasaunce with peramours; that
woll I refuse: in prencipall for drede of God, for knyghtes that bene adventures
[adventurous] sholde nat be advoutrers nothir lecherous, for than they be nat happy
nother fortunate unto the werrys' (ed. Vinaver, p. 270).

I may bot mourne vpon molde, as may þat much louyes.'
Sykande ho sweȝe doun and semly hym kyssed.

(1793–6)

["But I am answered indeed, so that it seems to me painful. Kiss me now
nicely, and I shall go away; I can but sorrow upon earth, as a maid who
loves much." Sighing she stooped down and pleasantly kissed him.]

This kiss, the second of the scene, marks the end of the lady's
'wowyng' (as Bercilak later describes it), but not of her testing. Here,
as at the end of the first temptation scene, she gets up from the bed
only to deliver a parting shot 'as ho stondes' (compare l. 1291). She
asks for a keepsake—any kind of gift, a glove would do. Her tone is
friendly and informal, with a lot of singular pronouns ('þy . . . þi
. . . þe'), as if confessing, confidentially, to her failure; but it wins
only one concession from Gawain—a single 'thou,' the only one he ever
uses to the lady (l. 1802). Otherwise his reply is much in the style of
his earlier refusals. In particular, there is the same polite, sophistical
play with values: nothing but the best is good enough to 'reward' the
lady (as if that were the point of a keepsake), and he, being 'an erande,'
has no 'menskful þingeȝ' with him. What he has (taking up the lady's
suggestion of a glove) is quite unworthy of her—and even of him:

Hit is not your honour to haf at þis tyme
A gloue for a garysoun of Gawayneȝ gifteȝ.

(1806–7)

[It is not to your honor to have at this time a glove for a keepsake, as a
gift of Gawain's.]

The touch of self-esteem in the last phrase is well-calculated: the lady
can hardly reject an argument which she herself has used on more
than one occasion.

The first part of the following stanza is devoted to the lady's un-
accepted offer of a rich gold ring with a precious stone in it. This
episode, besides 'leading up' in a general way to the offer and acceptance of the girdle, seems designed specifically to establish a point about
Gawain's motives there. As we shall see, the poet devotes a good deal
of attention, once Gawain has 'fallen,' to ensuring that the reader
understands what, morally speaking, he did and why he did it; and he
insists, among other things, that his hero was quite unmoved by the
costliness and beauty of the girdle. We are told this no less than three
times in the fourth fitt, once by the poet (ll. 2037–40), once by the

Green Knight (2367–8) and once by Gawain himself (2430–3). Gawain is not vain or covetous: he does not wear the lady's gift 'for wele' (2037, 2432). It seems clear, in retrospect at least, that the ring episode is designed to make the same point—to make sure in advance that the reader does not misunderstand the hero's motives. This explains the somewhat naïve stress on the costliness of the ring. It clears the ground. Anyone who refuses such a ring is immune from covetousness at least.

The importance of the scene's final episode—the turning-point of the poem—is marked from the outset. Up to this point in the castle scenes, the poet has been chary of any pointed allusion to the identity of the host; he has not, as it were, made any rhetorical capital out of it ('had Gawain but known . . .' etc.). So the occurrence of such an allusion, even though indirect, here in the description of the girdle which the lady produces from under her mantle, is doubly effective:

> Gered hit watჳ with grene sylke and with golde schaped.
>
> (1832)

> [It was fashioned of green silk, and adorned with gold.]

The Green Knight's characteristic combination of green and gold, reappearing thus unexpectedly, creates a powerful sense of threat and complicity (almost as in some of Henry James' novels); but it does not alert the hero, who again replies in his old style of polite refusal, falling back into his defensive role of 'trwe seruaunt.' The lady ripostes, still in their best chamber manner, by drawing his attention to another problem of value ('pris'):

> 'Now forsake ჳe þis silke,' sayde þe burde þenne,
> 'For hit is symple in hitself? And so hit wel semeჳ.
> Lo! so hit is littel, and lasse hit is worþy;
> Bot who-so knew þe costes þat knit ar þerinne,
> He wolde hit prayse at more prys, parauenture.'
>
> (1846–50)

> ["Now do you refuse this silk," said the lady then, "because it is simple in itself? And so it indeed seems. Lo! it is little, and smaller in worth; but whoever knew the qualities that are knit into it would esteem it at a greater value, perhaps."]

The casual tone is deceptive: the girdle is little and simple in itself, but it is perhaps ('parauenture') more valuable than it looks—for it has the power to protect its wearer from violent death.

It is a dramatic moment. After the subtle and elaborate manoeu-vrings which have gone before, the lady suddenly shifts her ground and makes a direct appeal to a passion which, under the circumstances, must be stronger than sexual desire—the passion for life. The appeal goes home:

> Þen kest þe knyȝt, and hit come to his hert,
> Hit were a juel for þe jopardé þat hym iugged were.
>
> (1855–6)

[Then pondered the knight, and it came into his heart; it would be a jewel for the peril that was assigned to him.]

Gawain first allows the lady to go on pressing him ('þulged with hir þrepe'), then accepts the gift and finally agrees not to reveal it to the host or anyone else 'for noȝte.' So, in order (as he thinks) to save his life, he incurs an obligation to the lady which is inconsistent with his obligations to her husband: he cannot now be true to both. How-ever we take this, it plainly involves some falling off from the standards of 'truth' represented in the pentangle passage. The exemplary knight, the mirror of Christian chivalry—developed in that passage out of the more ordinary 'good Gawain' of the first fitt—gives way here, for the first time, to human weakness. There is a powerful and ominous note of finality (deriving in part from confused suggestions of the betrayal of Christ—by Judas with a kiss and by Peter three times before cock-crow) in the closing lines of the stanza:

> He þonkked hir oft ful swyþe,
> Ful þro with hert and þoȝt.
> Bi þat on þrynne syþe
> Ho hatȝ kyst þe knyȝt so toȝt.
>
> (1866–9)

[He thanked her often very strongly, most earnestly with heart and thought. By this time she has kissed the bold knight three times.]

Structure and Symmetry in *Sir Gawain*

by *Donald R. Howard*

No one who reads *Sir Gawain and the Green Knight* fails to notice its elaborate, symmetrical structure. Everywhere in the poem is balance, contrast, and antithesis. Things are arranged in pairs—there are two New Year's days, two "beheading" scenes, two courts, two confessions; or in threes—three temptations, three hunts, three kisses, three strokes of the ax. These intricacies are unobtrusively integrated with events and themes; and perhaps just for that reason, critics have taken note of them only piecemeal and in passing, often with reference to the poem's mythic or symbolic content.[1] In what follows I intend to examine the narrative units based upon structural parallels in *Sir Gawain,* and to suggest in what way they coincide with the divisions of the poem marked by the ornamented and colored capitals of the manuscript. To do so, however, I shall have to turn first to the symbolism of the poem; for what I wish to argue is that its most protracted structural parallel depends upon the juxtaposition of two symbols, the shield and the girdle.

I

Everyone from Mary McCarthy to C. S. Lewis has expressed caveats about literary symbolism, and it is true, symbol-hunting is an easy

"Structure and Symmetry in Sir Gawain*" by Donald R. Howard. From* Speculum, *Vol. XXXIX (1964), 425–33. Copyright © 1964 by The Mediaeval Academy of America. Reprinted by permission of The Mediaeval Academy of America. Translations have been supplied.*

[1] Morton W. Bloomfield in *"Sir Gawain and the Green Knight:* An Appraisal," (*PMLA*, LXXVI [1961], 17) has pointed to the need for detailed analysis of the poem's structure. Some pertinent comments may be found in Charles Moorman, "Myth and Mediaeval Literature: *Sir Gawain and the Green Knight," Mediaeval Studies,* XVIII (1956), 164–69, and in Francis Berry, *"Sir Gawayne and the Grene Knight,"* in *The Age of Chaucer,* ed. Boris Ford (Pelican Books A290, 1954), pp. 152–55. For further references see the footnotes which follow.

game with no particular criteria of corrigibility. In the study of mediaeval literature there is the added problem of a vast body of symbolism based on the four-level method of interpreting Scripture.[2] It is
reassuring, therefore, to have at least one mediaeval work in which
the symbols are identified as such by the author. No one has ever
questioned the fact that the pentangle shield and the green girdle
in *Sir Gawain and the Green Knight* are symbols. They are neither
"Freudian" nor "patristic." Rather, the author tells us in ll. 619–665
what the pentangle means, and there is precedent in mediaeval lore
for that symbolic meaning. Likewise with the magic girdle, when
Gawain keeps it at the end of the poem he says in so many words
that it is to be a "syngne of my surfet" to remind him of the "faut
and þe fayntyse of þe flesche crabbed." [3]

Yet I think no one has examined the way in which these two symbols are juxtaposed and paired, so that their meaning, to use North-
rop Frye's language, comes about through the centripetal force of
their relationship within the whole literary structure.[4] Gawain's journey to the Green Chapel, we know, is made in two stages. Hence
there are two descriptions of the arming of the knight, one when he
leaves Arthur's court (ll. 536–669), the other when he leaves Bercilak's
castle (ll. 2011–41). The earlier passage begins with Gawain's statement of his indifference to his destiny—"Quat schuld I wonde?/Of
destinés derf and dere/What may mon do bot fonde?" (ll. 563–565);
it ends with the description of the shield. The later passage, however, ends with a description not of the shield but of the girdle, which
Gawain wears "to save himself."

Thus the girdle, within the symbolic structure of the poem, becomes a substitute for the shield. By shield I mean the shield itself,
not its painted allegory. Critics often treat the shield and its pen-

[2] With respect to *Sir Gawain*, see Hans Schnyder, *Sir Gawain and the Green
Knight: An Essay in Interpretation,* Cooper Monographs, 6 (Bern, 1961). While
Schnyder grants (p. 74) that "the poem does not simply consist of a series of
allegorical situations pedantically and painstakingly strung together," he treats
dozens of recondite symbols in the poem without ever acknowledging the humorous
tone, and devotes a chapter to the temptations without ever mentioning the girdle.

[3] ll. 2433–36. References are to the edition of J. R. R. Tolkien and E. V. Gordon
(Oxford, 1930).

[4] See *Anatomy of Criticism* (Princeton, 1957), pp. 82–94. That the shield and girdle
stand in relation to each other is recognized by Robert W. Ackerman, "Gawain's
Shield: Penitential Doctrine in *Gawain and the Green Knight,*" *Anglia,* LXXVI
(1958), 265, and by Richard H. Green, "Gawain's Shield and the Quest for Perfection," *ELH,* XXIX (1962), 137.

tangle device as a single object, which of course they are. Yet the symbolism of shield and girdle is symbolism of a different kind from that of the pentangle. The pentangle has an *assigned* symbolic value; it is put into the poem in order to stand for an abstraction, like Sansfoy and Sansloy, or Sin and Death. It tells us that Gawain is the "pentagonal man," the ideal knight.[5] The shield and girdle, however, take their symbolic meaning from the situation, the use they are put to, the attitudes and emotions which people show towards them, and their juxtaposition one against the other. They remain just as much girdle and shield as Desdemona's handkerchief remains a handkerchief, or Eve's apple an apple. While the pentangle is a painted sign —it appears on the knight's cote-armor as well as on his shield[6]— the shield and girdle are real objects, and function in the poem as living, articulate symbols, dynamically paired.

The pentangle shield of course evokes the chivalric ideal. As part of the knight's armor, it is not surprising that it has symbolic meaning, for a knight's garments and gear, like a priest's vestments, were often given symbolic values.[7] Yet the description of the arming of Sir Gawain gives no symbolic meaning to anything *but* the pentangle. All his articles of clothing and armor are described in the most worldly terms—they are of costly silk, of bright fur, of well-worked and highly polished steel adorned with gold. His helmet, the last garment he puts on (kissing it as a priest might kiss the stole), has a silk cover embroidered with the best gems and encircled with costly diamonds. His garments and armor are also *useful*—they are "alle þe godlych gere þat hym gayn schulde" (l. 584). The poet has concentrated all his powers on the lush description and saved the symbolism of moral values until the end, where it is more pointed and

[5] On the pentangle, see Vincent F. Hopper, *Medieval Number Symbolism* . . . , Columbia University Studies in English and Comparative Literature, 132 (New York, 1938), pp. 124–25, and Edgar de Bruyne, *Études d'esthétique médiévale*, II: *L'époque romane*, Rijksuniversiteit te Gent, Werken uitgegeven door de Faculteit van de Wijsbegeerte en Letteren, 98 (Bruges, 1946), pp. 349–50; also Green, pp. 129–35. On the shield, see Green, pp. 126–29 and Schnyder, pp. 53–4.

[6] See line 637.

[7] On the symbolism of the knight's garments, see Edgar Prestage, "The Chivalry of Portugal," in *Chivalry: A Series of Studies to Illustrate Its Historical Significance and Civilizing Influence*, ed. Edgar Prestage (New York, 1928), p. 145; A. T. Byles, "Medieval Courtesy Books and the Prose Romances of Chivalry," *ibid.*, p. 192; Sidney Painter, *French Chivalry: Chivalric Ideas and Practices in Mediaeval France* (Baltimore, 1940), pp. 83–4.

dramatic. By arranging his material in this way, he has underscored an essential fact: that a knight's valor is dependent on worldly means. The practice of chivalry presents the knight with the problem of using the world's goods for worldly ends and yet adopting those virtues which will keep him from loving the world itself.

After hearing Mass, Gawain puts on his helmet and takes up the shield (the manuscript at this point makes a subdivision with a colored capital).[8] On its inside is the image of the Blessed Virgin, which will remind Gawain of her five joys and so renew his courage. On its outside is the pentangle or "endless knot," representing Gawain's perfection in his five senses and his five fingers, his faith in the five wounds of Christ and the five joys of the Virgin, and his possession of the five knightly virtues—franchise, fellowship, purity, courtesy, and pity.[9] (These virtues, as Professor Engelhardt has shown,[10] correspond in a general way to the chivalric virtues of piety, valor, and courtesy, and so represent his religious, military, and courtly obligations.) Hence the shield, with its images on either side, functions in two ways—to the knight as a devotional reminder, to the world as an emblem of his inner moral perfection. It is at base a worldly object, a part of his warlike gear, designed at once to protect his body and remind him of his immortal soul, so that it suggests at once his knightly valor and his spiritual indifference to destiny. To the world, the shield shows what spiritual strength lies beneath Gawain's rich trappings; to Gawain, it shows what ultimate spiritual meaning lies beneath the world's bright lures. Yet it is to have this devotional and spiritual meaning precisely in those moments when he is most the knight, when he is most given to worldly deeds and most reliant upon the shield as a made object. It thus points to the proper attitude for a knight: to be indifferent to one's life in the world and yet preserve it, to use the world well and yet love it little.[11]

*   *   *

[8] See Tolkien and Gordon, p. viii.

[9] Ackerman (*Anglia*, LXXVI, 254–65) suggests that the reference to the five wits would have called up fourteenth-century writings on auricular confession, so that the passage is consistent with the later theme of penitence.

[10] George J. Engelhardt, "The Predicament of Gawain," *Modern Language Quarterly*, XVI (1955), 218–25.

[11] On the Christian and "otherworldly" aspects of the chivalric code, see Painter, Chap. 3, and F. Warre Cornish, *Chivalry* (London, 1908), pp. 218–19. See also Henry Osborn Taylor, *The Mediaeval Mind: A History of the Development of Thought and Emotion in the Middle Ages*, 2 vols. (London, 1930), I, 545–51.

After the temptations, when Gawain is ready to leave the castle for the Green Chapel, the poet again describes the arming of the knight. This time, however, he says nothing about the shield; instead, he ends by explaining why Gawain wears the girdle:

> Bot wered not þis ilk wyȝe for wele þis gordel,
> For pryde of þe pendaunteȝ, þaȝ polyst þay were,
> And þaȝ þe glyterande golde glent vpon endeȝ,
> Bot for to sauen hymself, when suffer hym byhoued,
> To byde bale withoute dabate of bronde hym to were
>   oþer knyffe.

(ll. 2037–2042)

[But this same man did not wear this girdle for its value, for pride in its pendants, polished though they were, and though the glittering gold glinted at its ends, but to save himself, when he must suffer, wait for disaster without resistance of sword or knife to defend himself.]

As the shield is emblematic of Gawain's knightly virtue, the girdle is emblematic of his fault. The whole movement of the story hangs upon his yielding to temptation, accepting the girdle, and having his failing revealed to him. In the end, Gawain himself makes the girdle a symbol of his "surfet" and of the weakness of the flesh. Now a girdle was an ordinary article of clothing, a belt or cincture from which one hung objects like keys or a purse. Because of its function, it was a convenient symbol for worldliness—the Oxford English Dictionary in fact reports such a metaphorical usage in the fifteenth century. *This* girdle, however, has the added lure of being rich and finely wrought in its own right: it is made of green silk, embroidered about the edges, and hung with pendants of highly polished gold.[12] More than that, it has powers of its own—not merely an emblematic meaning, like that of the shield's device, but remarkable "costes þat knit ar þerinne" (l. 1849), magical properties to save the wearer from being slain. The author carefully reminds us that Gawain accepts the girdle for these powers, not for its richness. He goes so far as to tell us what the knight thought before accepting it:

> Þen kest þe knyȝt, and hit come to his hert,
> Hit were a juel for þe jopardé þat hym iugged were,
> When he acheued to þe chapel his chek for to fech;

---

[12] See ll. 1830–33, 2037–39, 2430–32.

Myȝt he haf slypped to be vnslayn, þe sleȝt were
noble.

(ll. 1855–58)

[Then pondered the knight, and it came into his heart; it would be a
jewel for the peril that was assigned to him when he reached the chapel
to obtain his destiny; if he might escape unslain, it would be a noble
device.]

And Gawain, when he proposes to wear it as a memento of his failing,
himself denies any interest in either its worth or its beauty:

'Bot your gordel' quoþ Gawayn 'God yow forȝelde!
Þat wyl I welde wyth good wylle, not for þe wynne
golde,
Ne þe saynt, ne þe sylk, ne þe syde pendaundes,
For wele ne for worchyp, ne for þe wlonk werkkeȝ,
Bot in syngne of my surfet I schal se hit ofte,
When I ride in renoun, remorde to myseluen
Þe faut and þe fayntyse of þe flesche crabbed,
How tender hit is to entyse teches of fylþe . . .

(ll. 2429–36)

["But for your girdle," said Gawain, "may God reward you! That will
I gladly possess, not for the lovely gold, nor the material, nor the silk,
nor the long pendants, not for value nor for honor, nor for its splendid
workmanship, but as a sign of my transgression I shall often see it, when
I ride in glory, and call to mind with remorse the faultiness and the
frailty of the perverse flesh, how liable it is to take stains of filth . . ."]

Gawain has taken the girdle, then, not to own it for its value or wear
it for its beauty, but simply to save his life.[13] It is as worldly an object, and used for as worldly an end as the shield; but unlike the
shield, it is magical, it is used solely for a selfish reason, and its acceptance requires that he act dishonorably either to the lady or her
husband if he is to keep it. He is guilty not because he desires "to
sauen hymself," but because in order to do so he uses worldly means
in the wrong way.

Even after he has taken the girdle, however, the knight continues

---

[13] John Burrow in "The Two Confession Scenes in *Sir Gawain and the Green
Knight*" (*Modern Philology*, LVII [1959], 73–9) has pointed out that Gawain twice
confesses to covetousness (ll. 2374–86, 2507–08) but his extravagance is corrected and
the sin specifically denied (ll. 2366–68, 2429–32).

to profess submission to God's will. When tempted by his guide to
flee he declares, "Ful wel con dryʒtyn schape/His seruaunteʒ for to
saue" (ll. 2138–39), and again, "I wyl nauþer grete ne grone;/To God-
deʒ wylle I am ful bayn,/And to hym I haf me tone" (ll. 2157–59).
So, when he sees the Green Chapel, he says, "Let God worche! . . .
My lif þaʒ I forgoo,/Drede dotʒ me no lote" (ll. 2208–11). In these
utterances we must not think him hypocritical. While he has taken
the girdle and presumably held some hope for its efficacy, he has not
deserted, but compromised, the chivalric ideal and its religious re-
quirements. He is, in fact, never wholly sure of the girdle's powers. At
the first stroke of the ax he flinches; and on the third stroke, when
his neck is nicked, he bounds up and throws into place—his shield.

Gawain's indifference to "destinés derf and dere" is, we need to remember, the self-abnegation not of the cloistered monk but of the
active knight. "What may mon do bot fonde?" (l. 565) he had asked
—what can one do but *try*. He is admirably suited to put his destiny
to the test: he is devoted to the articles of faith and has the virtues
appropriate to the ideal Christian knight. The problem is to maintain the fine balance between this religious ethos and the unavoidable
necessity of using worldly means to preserve life and accomplish
knightly deeds. Hence he accepts the girdle not for any active pride
which revolts against God, nor for avarice, nor covetousness, nor for
vainglory, but for instinctive self-preservation, the central, involun-
tary worldliness of fallen man, through which even the best is easily
tempted. This perfectly understandable weakness, however, leads him
into other transgressions—the breaking of his oath to the lord, the
false confession, the last failure of courtesy to the Green Knight.
Once he has upset that finely balanced indifference to the world,
those of the chivalric virtues which govern worldly action become
in part unattainable. The poem suggests in this way how the worldly
aims of chivalry and the other-worldly aims of the Christian life are
ideally interrelated, but, for fallen man, potentially incompatible.

II

The poet suggested these distinctions by treating as symbols articles
which were naturally part of his story. The girdle and shield are juxtaposed as two kinds of worldliness: the girdle an illicit and self-cen-

tered means of holding on to life; the shield an allowable, self-ab-
negating use of the world's goods in the service of the highest Christian ideals. These two symbols, paired so that they reflect the moral
choice which confronts the hero, initiate two sequences which form a
major structural parallel in the poem. The main action, beginning
with Gawain's departure in the second division, falls into two stages
—the events at the castle, and those at the Green Chapel.[14] The one
comprises Sections II and III; the other, Section IV. No one, I think,
has noticed that these two sequences are matched by an elaborate
parallelism. The same kinds of events, in exactly the same order, occur in either part, and they center upon the three temptations in the
first sequence and the three strokes of the ax in the second, with a
confession following in each. These parallel contrasts are used artisti-
cally to distinguish Gawain's temptation and fall from his punish-
ment and pardon. We shall see this best if we represent the contrasts in diagram:

Sections II–III	*Section IV*
(1) Arming of the knight, and description of the shield (ll. 536–669)	Arming of the knight, and description of the girdle (ll. 1998–2041)
(2) Journey to the castle (ll. 670–762)	Journey to the Green Chapel (ll. 2069–2159)
(3) Description of the castle (ll. 763–810)	Description of the Green Chapel (ll. 2160–2211)
(4) Three temptations (ll. 1126–1869)	Three strokes of the ax (ll. 2212–2330)
(5) Confession to priest (ll. 1876–1884)	Confession to Green Knight (ll. 2378–2438)

This structural design coincides with the four manuscript divisions
marked by ornamented capitals, the four "sections" of the poem ob-

---

[14] Dale B. J. Randall in "A Note on Structure in *Sir Gawain and the Green
Knight*" (*Modern Language Notes*, LXXII [1957], 161–63) points out also that the
Green Knight is the fiendish challenger at the beginning and end, but the genial
host in the middle. The three parts correspond to those I have outlined—the "prologue," and the two parts of the major action. Such a triple structure was pointed
out by Sylvan Barnet ("A Note on the Structure of *Sir Gawain and the Green
Knight*," *MLN*, LXXI [1956], 319), who remarks on its consistency with the pattern
hunt-temptation-hunt, with the three temptations, three hunts, three strokes of the
ax, and so on.

served in editions. Now the last three of these are subdivided by small ornamented capitals, so that the whole falls into nine units.[15] These nine units seem to be based on a principle of suspense; they mark off blocks of information. The four major divisions, on the other hand, mark the major episodes of the story—the opening scene, with the beheading episode and challenge; the passing of a year, and Gawain's journey to the castle; the temptations; and the second "beheading" scene, followed by the explanation and Gawain's return to court. The opening scene is kept as a single unit with no internal division—a kind of prologue to the mission which Gawain must undertake. The work begins and ends with a reference to the fall of Troy and the founding of Britain, so that the events at Arthur's court are seen in the perspective of history as a point out of the past to which the reader draws up close and then away.[16] This sense of the sweep of time is matched within the poem by the lines on the passing of the year, at the beginning of the second division (ll. 491–535), which divide the prologue from the main action—the first New Year's feast with its beheading episode from the journey which Gawain must make a year later.

The second division of the poem is therefore a kind of intermezzo between the challenge and Gawain's journey. It comprises the description of the year's passing, Gawain's preparations to leave, the description of his armor with the passage on the pentangle, his voyage through the wilderness, and his arrival at the castle. The smaller capitals of the manuscript make two divisions within it, one beginning with the description of the shield (l. 619), the other with his arrival at the castle (l. 763). In the castle, a great dinner is set with many dishes and fine sauces, which Gawain calls a feast; it is a fish dinner, though, since Christmas Eve is a fast day, and he is drolly reminded that these culinary splendors are a penance—"Þis penaunce now ȝe take,/And eft hit schal amende" (ll. 897–98). After dinner the company hears evensong, and in the chapel Gawain sees for the first time the beautiful young lady with her ugly, aged companion.[17] On the

---

[15] See Laurita Lyttleton Hill, "Madden's Divisions of *Sir Gawain* and the 'Large Initial Capitals' of *Cotton Nero A.x.*," *Speculum*, XXI (1946), 67–71. Mrs. Hill argues that the size of the capitals is without significance.

[16] Randall, pp. 161–63, points out that the frame at the beginning and end reverses the order of the three elements—"þe sege," Brutus, and Arthur's court.

[17] For the principle of description by contrast in this passage, see Derek A. Pearsall, "Rhetorical 'Descriptio' in *Sir Gawain and the Green Knight*," *Modern Language Review*, L (1955), 129–34.

next day there is a true Christmas feast; after it Gawain learns that the Green Chapel is nearby, and agrees that while waiting to leave he will exchange what he wins in the castle for what the lord wins hunting. Throughout, there is a fine balance of contraries: the revolution of the seasons, the warlike shield and its religious emblem, the unpleasant journey and the agreeable life of the castle, fasting and feasting, youth and age, beauty and ugliness, and at last the agreement to give what each has gained.

This tendency to match and contrast things is a dominant feature of the poem's style. It is, with respect to the purely verbal element, a feature encouraged by alliterative verse; a dozen examples come to mind—"bliss and blunder," "brittened and brent," "stad and stoken." And as we have seen, it sustains the structural unity not only in the two beheading scenes juxtaposed at beginning and end, but in the parallels, diagrammed above, between the events at the castle (Sections II–III) and those at the chapel (Section IV). These parallels contribute to the almost ritual symmetry of the whole, and they give to the later sequence a dream-like aura of familiarity. Each of them contrasts in its own way, and each contrast contributes to the mystery and wonder of the final scene:

(1) In both parts, the arming of the knight before the journey is described in detail. In the earlier passage, the description ends with the lines on the pentangle shield. But when Gawain leaves the castle for the Green Chapel, the shield is not mentioned; instead the passage ends with a description of the girdle and a reminder that he is wearing it not for avarice or vainglory, but only to save his life.

(2) In both parts he must undertake a journey. In the earlier journey there is positive danger from beasts and giants; there is cold, and hardship. In the shorter journey to the Green Chapel there are no physical dangers, but there is a spiritual one: his guide tempts him to flee. The description of the mist which hovers about the place and of the streams flowing through it creates an atmosphere of eerie uncertainty, very different from the explicit perils of the earlier passage: here, the perils are to come at the *end* of the journey.

(3) In both parts, the building is described as the knight comes upon it. The castle is on a knoll, surrounded by a park, and is built in the very newest style of late fourteenth-century architecture.[18] It is

[18] See Tolkien and Gordon, pp. 94–5.

so new, and so idealized, that it seems almost illusory; its pinnacles, the author tells us, seemed as if cut out of paper (l. 802).[19] The Green Chapel, on the other hand, is ancient and gnarled, in part subterranean—such a place as the devil at midnight would say his matins in—like a cave or the crevice of an old crag, overgrown with grass. It is at the fork of a roaring stream, and the air is split with the ominous, and comic, whirring of a grindstone.

(4) The three temptations are of course paralleled by the three strokes of the ax. The temptations are carried out with an exuberant humor in which the daily hunting and the exchange of winnings serve as humorous parallels. The hunts themselves contrast with the temptations in intensity and aggressiveness, and the animals hunted suggest those qualities which Gawain must conquer—timidity, ferocity, and cunning.[20] The relation between Gawain and the lady reverses the courtly love code, in which the God of Love was said to be irresistible; in fact, in *Sir Gawain,* the lady offers to be the knight's servant (l. 1240).[21] The enviable but ridiculous position of the hero was a familiar one, to be sure, but it is heightened by the ritual exchanges. The kisses increase in number daily. The whole is recounted in a tone of suppressed mirth; while there is great suspense over the outcome of the temptations, the reader is encouraged to feel that he really knows what is going on. The lord's replies on receiving the kisses are richly ambiguous, for it is never wholly clear whether or not he knows what his wife has been up to. And the romping style of the passage makes the reader feel that he knows something of the *kind* of outcome, though he knows no details.

But at the Green Chapel, the three strokes of the ax are short and suspenseful. We know something is going to happen; we hear a noise, *as if* someone were grinding a scythe! But when Gawain gets under

[19] See Robert W. Ackerman, " 'Pared out of Paper': *Gawain* 802 and *Purity* 1408," *Journal of English and Germanic Philology,* LVI (1957), 410–17. Ackerman shows that the line refers to a custom of serving food on festive occasions covered or crowned with paper decorations in such shapes as that of a castle. Cf. Chaucer, *Parson's Tale,* X. 444.

[20] For the latter point, see John Speirs, *Medieval English Poetry: The Non-Chaucerian Tradition* (London, 1957), pp. 236–37. On the hunting scenes, see Henry L. Savage, *The "Gawain"-Poet: Studies in His Personality and Background* (Chapel Hill, 1956), pp. 31–48.

[21] On the treatment of the situation here as a reversal of courtly love, see J. F. Kiteley, "The *De Arte Honeste Amandi* of Andreas Capellanus and the Concept of Courtesy in *Sir Gawain and the Green Knight,*" *Anglia,* LXXIX (1961), 7–16.

the ax, we are completely in the dark. Even when his neck is nicked on the third stroke and he bounds up in self-defense, we are puzzled. When he accepted the girdle, we knew exactly what had happened; here, we are more confused than ever. We know the facts, but they make no sense.

(5) The explanation of course follows at once. As soon as Gawain's fault is revealed to him he flares up at the knight, flinging the girdle at him. Then he confesses his fault. This confession, as John Burrow has shown, parallels his confession to the priest after Gawain has taken the girdle. That earlier confession was really invalid; but in the second confession (though made to the Green Knight) he is genuinely contrite, he makes an honest confession (ll. 2379–86), he promises to do better (ll. 2387–88), and of course he does public penance by wearing the girdle. The court's judgment of his sin, however, is far less severe than his own—he twice confesses covetousness, although this is specifically denied in the poem. He wears the girdle as a sign of the weakness of the flesh, and the rest of the court join him in wearing a green band across their chests. Agreeing to do so, the king comforts him and the rest laugh.

This analysis of the narrative structure indicates that the significant manuscript divisions are the ornamented capitals which mark the four major divisions. The five small capitals which mark subdivisions do not systematically correspond to narrative units. They seem to serve for emphasis, and were probably placed in accord with the author's —or scribe's—sense of dramatic rhythm. One precedes the description of the shield (l. 619); another marks Gawain's arrival at the castle (l. 763). In the third section, one marks the beginning of the second temptation (l. 1421), and another follows Gawain's confession (l. 1893). In the fourth section, there is a small capital at the beginning of the "beheading" scene (l. 2259). If we divided the poem into nine sections (without regard to the size of the capitals), its structure and symmetry would be obscured. All of this lends significance to a fact which has generally been ignored: at each of the three internal divisions marked by the larger capitals, the scribe has left one ruled space, and through each of these spaces the illuminator has extended the red ornamentation across the page in an identical design. There is no similar spacing or ornamentation elsewhere within the text of *Sir Gawain* or of the other three poems preserved in the same manuscript.

This elaborate parallelism, with its multiple contrasts, helps produce the game-like, ironic tone of *Sir Gawain*. Its effect is comic. The ritual balance of incidents does, in the end, what comedy always does —it purges extremes of conduct and brings the reader comfortably back to a norm; it restores the *status quo*. Gawain returns to the starting-place, and, however chastened, is greeted with laughter which dispels his sobriety. The symbolism of shield and girdle suggests an essential and inescapable conflict between chivalry and Christianity; but this conflict is treated throughout in a spirit of amused and ironic detachment, as if the poet meant to suggest that these contrarieties of mediaeval thought, being irreconcilable, should be taken in good humor as a condition of life in an imperfect world. The mysterious and marvellous, which in tragedy remain ultimately incomprehensible, are here explained rationally away; we are asked not so much to *feel* the hero's experience as to think about it, to understand. The symmetrical world of the poem is at once unreal and substantial— far in the past and idealized, and yet plainly the world of real human conduct, of uncertainty and self-deception. It is too neatly balanced to be like the flux of history itself, yet it is an unpredictable world full of surprises; and, from the long view, it is ordered and right.

The Criticism of Style

by Marie Borroff

The impression of style is, properly speaking, an impression of the use of language rather than of language itself. The use of language in turn, considered in relation to the occasion or mode of discourse, implies the character, in the broadest sense, of the speaker. In works of narrative poetry the speaker figures as the "I" through whose consciousness the events making up the plot are mediated to us. This narrating "I" is, like the persons of the action, a fictional being, and he is created by the implications of the poet's language. His character includes such traits as his formality or informality of manner, his social class and degree of culture, his technical knowledge, and the attitudes—approval or disapproval, sympathy or detachment, humor or solemnity, and so on—which he exhibits toward the subject matter of his narration. The style of the poem is thus the characteristic or effective way in which the story is told, and for the purposes of stylistic criticism, the broad outline of events is the material with relation to which stylistic choice is exercised. It does not matter that the poet may in fact have invented or modified some of the events themselves. Thus, even if the Gawain-poet was not the first to combine the "temptation" and "beheading game" stories, he seems to have originated that alternation of temptation and hunting scenes which contributes importantly to the effectiveness of the poem. Given an event as material, the poet must devise a succession of details as a means of narrating it. As an example we may take the coming of the lady of the castle to Gawain's bedroom on the first morning. This event could have been

"The Criticism of Style" by Marie Borroff. From Chapter 4 of Sir Gawain and the Green Knight: A Stylistic and Metrical Study, Yale Studies in English, Vol. 152 (New Haven and London: Yale University Press, 1962), pp. 91–94, 100, 102–105, 110–12, 115–18, 120, 128–29. The original footnotes have been omitted, and a translation has been supplied. Copyright © 1962 by Yale University. Reprinted by permission of the publisher.

treated in four or five lines; actually, it takes up sixteen (1179–94). Gawain lies in a fine bed, under a handsome coverlet; it is late, and daylight shines on the walls; he hears in half sleep a little noise at the door; he lifts his head, opens the curtain, and peers warily out; he sees that it is the lady; she closes the door after her stealthily and moves toward the bed; he becomes embarrassed; he lies down and pretends to sleep; she steps silently to the bed, lifts the curtain, comes inside, sits softly down, and stays there, waiting for him to awaken. These details, aside from the words and metrical patterns in which they are expressed, constitute an aspect of the style of the passage; they are characteristic and effective both in their abundance and in their content. The narrator envisages the action with characteristic interest and intensity, dwelling imaginatively on it as a series of precisely differentiated stages. This mode of perception results in a retarded pace, which in turn brings about an appropriate enhancement of suspense. It is, further, both characteristic and effective that the narrator sees the action from two complementary points of view: first, that of Gawain inside the curtains (1182–90); then that of the lady, whom Gawain can no longer see (1191–94); then again that of Gawain (1195 ff.). The skill of the poet can thus be appreciated in part if the details of narrative content are understood. And the historical study of style will have justified itself if through its findings we can see something of the artistry of the language in which that content is expressed.

Our study of words and phrases in *Gawain* included a survey of their use in other alliterative poems belonging to the same stylistic tradition. As a result of this comparative examination, we can distinguish two aspects of the personality and character of the narrating "I." Certain traits—those implied by the traditional features of the style of alliterative poetry—are his by convention, *qua* narrator of an alliterative romance. Other traits—those implied by the poet's modification of the traditional style and his use of it for the purposes of this particular poem—are his as an individual. As we have seen, the traditional practice of referring to the persons of the narrative by now one, now another of a group of synonyms expressing class status tends in itself to elevate the style, regardless of the value of the particular words of the synonym group. This effect manifests itself for the reader as the narrator's dignity of manner, the solemnity of his attitude toward his subject. This manner and this attitude, then, are among his traits, but they are common to all narrators of alliterative romance and are expected of him by virtue of his role. The narrator's traditional attitude is further implied by his frequent use of adjectives imputing extraordinary, larger-than-life qualities—of excellence and splendor, joy and grief, courtesy and prowess, courage and strength, danger and hardship, according to the subject matter of the passage in question. Again, the effect of this feature of style is independent of the stylistic status of the particular adjectives used. Finally, the archaic and poetic elements of the traditional vocabulary of alliterative poetry serve to elevate the style further. Since such words are remote from the familiar and trivial associations of everyday life, they imply the speaker's idealization of the subject matter. To call Gawain a *haþel* or a *burne,* rather than a *kniȝt* or *lorde,* is to envisage him in lofty terms. The use of the archaic and poetic vocabulary also serves to make the character of the narrator more impressive, for it implies his knowledge of the tradition and its values, his status as an authority.

Both the traditional and the individual in the style of *Sir Gawain and the Green Knight* may be illustrated by a passage from the opening section of the poem, stanza 3 of Part I . . .

Although its vocabulary is largely of an everyday character, the effect of the passage is nonetheless one of elevation and dignity. The few elevated words and meanings it contains serve to enhance this effect, but are not in themselves sufficient to cause it. Of greater importance for the criticism of style is the group of qualitative adjectives, which also expresses the most important meanings. Examination of the content of the passage shows that the subjective preponderates over the factual throughout. In twenty-three lines we learn that King Arthur held a Christmas feast at Camelot with the knights of the Round Table and their ladies; there were jousts and carols; the feast lasted fifteen days, with joyful clamor by day and dancing by night. The rest is idealization, much of it taking the form of explicit judgments expressed by the narrator with intensity and conviction. Statements of fact are expanded by repetition and emphasis rather than by a variety of illustrative detail. . . .

The passage comes to a climax of intensity in lines 50–55. The narrator affirms that the court lived at Camelot "with all þe wele of þe worlde"—not all the goods of the world but all that is good, as defined in the preceding lines. The *þay* of line 50 is expanded in the three lines that follow into *knyȝteȝ, ladies,* and *kyng,* each preceded by a stock epithet of compliment traditionally linked with it in alliteration.

The suspension of syntax and the elaborate parallelism of lines 51–53 give the lines elevation and dignity, while at the same time they retain their quality of simple and direct affirmation. In assessing the total effect, here as elsewhere in the poem, we cannot overlook an additional point. For the ear educated in the stylistic tradition of alliterative poetry, the closing of each line with a word traditionally used in final position constitutes a recognizable cadence, a satisfaction of conscious or unconscious expectation similar to that produced in rhymed verse by the second rhyming word.

The sequence of long lines [37–54] reaches its conclusion in another summarizing statement, in which the youth of the court is now emphasized, with implications that will be discussed later. The wheel recapitulates the content of the preceding group of lines in terse and dignified fashion. It concludes with a pleonastic linking of qualitative adjective and phrase expressing place which appears thoroughly traditional and might easily be passed over without a second glance. But so far as I have been able to discover, "hardy on hille" 59 does not occur elsewhere in the alliterative and rhymed romances. On reflection, the reason for this is obvious: "hardiness" is not properly demonstrated "on hill"—i.e. in castle; it is demonstrated in the field. One is reminded of Sir Thopas, who was "fair and gent / In bataille and in tourneyment." But the effect here is certainly not parody; neither is it clearly ironic. The *here* is called *hardy*, as the *ledeʒ* are said in line 38 to be "of þe best," not in contradiction to particular actions or events, but in abstraction from them. The narrator does not question the traditional hardihood of Arthur's knights; his affirmation in lines 58–59 is straightforward. But there remains a nuance that seems inescapable. The traditional warlike virtues of the group of retainers exist in isolation, at least for the moment, from external hostility or challenge. . . .

King Arthur's refusal to take his place at the table is reported by the narrator in a way that deserves close attention. The gesture itself is, of course, part of the tradition. The narrator does not simply explain it, he overexplains it, giving it two motives, the first of which is not traditional. The youthful king is active and restless, even a little childish; he does not like to remain seated for a long time. The second motive, the traditional one, is carefully differentiated from the first: "& also anoþer maner meued him eke, / Þat he þurʒ nobelay had nomen." His behavior is also a sort of grand gesture, but its impressiveness as a gesture is diminished by its previous association with sheer boyish temperament. The treatment of the same material in *La Queste del Saint Graal* affords an illuminating contrast. Here, owing to his happiness at the return to the court of Sir Gawain, Sir Bors, and Sir Lionel, Arthur forgets that he must wait for an adventure to present itself before joining in the feast. He is reminded by Sir Kay that he should not sit down. The custom is thus depicted as involving a degree of self-denial on the king's part, rather than according with his natural inclinations.

The combination of the traditional qualitative adjective *stif* and the phrase *in stalle,* used both in line 104 of the wheel "He stiȝtleȝ stif in stalle" and in the first of the long lines of stanza 6 "Thus þer stondes in stale þe stif kyng his-seluen," appears to have been devised by the *Gawain*-poet for use in this episode. It is modeled on a number of traditional phrases. "Stif in stalle" is reminiscent of "stiff in stour" (with variants "stithe, sterne in stour"), which in turn has parallels in other phrases such as "bolde in batell," "felle in fight." *In stalle* is also parallel in position with *in halle* (102), with which it rhymes. These parallels suggest that *in stalle* means "in (his) place" rather than, or perhaps as well as, "in a standing position." Thus "stif in stalle" also suggests the traditional phrase "still in stede" ("stead, place"). (With 104 "He stiȝtleȝ stif in stalle," we may compare 2213a "Who stiȝtleȝ in þis sted?") The use of *stif* in combination with *stalle* and *stonde* insidiously robs it of its force as a traditional adjective of compliment to warlike virtues. Even more insidiously, it results in suggestions of unheroic woodenness and rigidity. As an epithet in the phrase "þe stif kyng," imputing qualities known to be characteristic of the person, *stif* adds solemnity of tone; in this context the solemnity of tone is meaningless. The traditional attitude of the narrator toward Arthur, as implied by the adjective, is maintained, one might say, solely "by courtesy." Whatever implications of boldness and inflexibility of will the descriptive reference might have carried are considerably diminished by the line that follows, in which we learn that the king was "talkkande bifore þe hyȝe table of trifles full hende" (108).

* * *

The entrance on the scene of the Green Knight is brilliantly handled. Lines 136–50, like the lines analyzed earlier, are composed in the traditional style of alliterative poetry, although they are somewhat less conventional in phraseology. The words used in the two passages are similar; the proportion of traditional poetic words is small in both, and there is in both a small group of obscure words which turn out to be either distinctively poetic (*rekenly, fade*) or distinctively colloquial (*glaum, enker*), so far as the available evidence enables us to determine. But the two passages differ significantly in effect, and the tradition is utilized in the later passage in a different way. . . .

In the first direct reference to the Green Knight ["Þer hales in at þe halle dor an aghlich mayster," 136] both the noun and the verb have implications of great interest. A priori, the logical choice for the noun might have seemed to be *wyȝt*. In Middle English this word had not only the meaning "a human being, man or woman" (*OED* s.v. *wight* sb. sense 2)—it is used by the poet to refer to the lady in line 1792— but "a living being in general" (s.v. sense 1); and it was often applied to supernatural beings (sense 1b). But *mayster*, the poet's actual choice, is certainly much better. As was pointed out above, *mayster* is used in alliterative poetry to refer to men, as a rule to men who are not warriors. But in addition to this general meaning, it has a host of more specific meanings which *wyȝt* does not have and which give it positive suggestions of great value. It differs, in fact, from all other words referring to persons in its associations with practical superiority, authority, and dominating or manipulating roles of various sorts in the real world. *Master* was used in the language of everyday communication to refer to persons having authority or competence not only in learning (*OED* s.v. *master* sb.¹ sense 12) but in such realms as government (sense 1), seamanship (sense 2), carpentry (cf. sense 14), and so on. (Cf. also sense 7: "One who has the power to control, use, or dispose of something at will.") The word thus leaves the Green Knight's identity open to doubt as *kniȝt* would not have done, while strongly implying the domineering role he is to play in the episode that follows.

The use of *hales* in this line, as in line 458, is comparatively rare in alliterative poetry. Of the meanings cited by the *OED* (s.v. *hale* v.¹), the closest is "to move along as if drawn or pulled . . . hasten, rush; spec. of a ship, to proceed before the wind with sails set" (sense 4). *Gawain* 136 is cited; the other uses all refer to ships. *Hale* also had the meaning "to flow, run down in a large stream," as in *Pearl* 125, and in this meaning survives in modern Scots and Northern dialects (s.v. sense 4b). Colloquial status for the nautical meaning is evidenced by the seventeenth- and eighteenth-century quotations in the *OED*.

The metaphorical use of *hale* for the coming of the Green Knight on his horse thus suggests powerful and continuous motion.

Assuming that style in narrative poetry manifests itself as the narrating "I"—the fictional being, implied by the language of the poem, by whom the events are reported—let us assess the role of the narrator of *Gawain* in the Challenge Episode, beginning with a summary of the events themselves. The Green Knight rushes into the court during the banquet and opens parley rudely, demanding to know which of those present is the king. The court is frightened at his supernatural appearance, but Arthur speaks. The challenge is presented and at first the court is silent. At this the Green Knight jeers; then Arthur accepts the challenge, but Gawain requests that he be allowed to take his place. The request is granted and he beheads the Knight, who picks up his head and departs, after explaining how Gawain is to go about finding him in a year's time.

Given these events as the material of the story, the particular form they will take—and this is true of all reporting, whether in life or in fiction—will depend on who is narrating them, his attitudes, his interests, and his sympathies. In addition it will depend on the way his mind and imagination work: any story can be told by one person methodically, by another in random fashion, by one person in detail, by another sketchily, and so on. The events, as mediated by the narrator, cease to be material; they are realized. Story becomes plot. The story of the Challenge Episode could be made into a number of different plots. It could, for example, be treated as an adventure in which the courage and courtesy of Arthur's court were demonstrated in an encounter with the supernatural. This statement, however, would constitute an inaccurate summary of the plot as we have it in *Gawain*. Rather, the Challenge Episode appears to us as a series of humiliations and discomfitures for the court which we feel as more comic than tragic. Despite the fact that the challenge is successfully met, the Green Knight departs from the scene as the victor in a kind of psychological warfare.

His overwhelming presence throughout the episode results in part from the simple fact that whereas he is described at length and in the minutest detail, neither Arthur nor any of his knights is described at all. The only detail of personal description prior to the entrance of the Green Knight is the reference to Guenevere's *yȝen gray* (82). Five lines plus the bob are devoted to the canopy and carpets surrounding her, and a little later on, nine lines plus the bob to the dishes served at the banquet. But the narrator goes into a lavish account of the Green Knight's size, figure, dress, accouterments, horse, coiffure, beard, and ax. It is much as if, in a group painting, one figure were drawn in the style of a Dürer engraving and the others sketched in a few lines. The Green Knight continues to receive the largest share of the narrator's attention throughout the events that follow. The fact that he has much more to say than anyone else aids in making his presence powerfully felt. This, of course, is not the narrator's responsibility (he reports all speeches verbatim); but the actions and gestures of the Green Knight are also given much more space than those of Arthur and the court.

After the challenge is delivered, for example, the narrator begins by telling of the reaction of the assembly:

> If he hem stowned vpon fyrst, stiller were þanne
> Alle þe hered-men in halle, þe hyȝ & þe loȝe
>
> (301–02)

[If he had astonished them at first, even quieter were then all the retainers in the hall, both the high and the low.]

There follow six lines of description, leading to the jeering speech which in a sense constitutes the climax of the episode: we are told how the Green Knight rolled his eyes, bent his brows, and wagged his beard and coughed as a preliminary to speaking. When Arthur accepts the challenge, two lines describe his handling of the ax (330–31), but these are followed by six lines plus the bob, describing the Green Knight's bold confrontation of the expected blow. When Gawain in his turn takes the ax and accomplishes the beheading, four lines are devoted to the Green Knight's gestures of preparation (417–20), six to Gawain's act of striking (421–26), but thirty-three (427–59) to the Green Knight's actions after the head falls. The picking up of the head, the final instructions, and the departure could have been dealt with in half as much space; instead, the narrator tells us of the rolling of the head among the beholders' feet, the glistening of the blood on the green clothing, the "ugly body that bled," and the head's lifting up its eyelids and "speaking with its mouth." The Green Knight continues to dominate the scene ("Moni on of hym had doute," 442) even though the blow he requested has been struck; and the loss of his head is, in fact, dealt with in the narration in such a way that through it he becomes more terrifying than ever. The king and Gawain begin to laugh (463–64) only after the sound of the green horse's hoofs has died away.

The material of the narrative, from the beginning of the poem on, is presented in such a way that certain relationships are tacitly emphasized, those which in another treatment of the same material might have been played down or suppressed altogether. One such relationship appears in what may be considered the first discomfiture of the court by the Green Knight, a discomfiture made possible by the fact that the king is not in his place at table. The narrator's account of the reasons for this behavior has been discussed in detail, and it has been shown that he takes pains to emphasize the part played in it by sheer youthful restlessness. Because Arthur is not in his place, the Green Knight can ask "Wher is þe gouernour of þis gyng?" (224–25) instead of greeting the head of the household as a preliminary to the delivery of the challenge. His question implies, moreover, that the king does not stand out from the rest in appearance or manner. And it is ambiguously, if not rudely, worded (*gyng* is cited by the *OED* from early Middle English on not only in the meaning "the retinue of a great personage" but "in depreciatory sense: a crew, rabble," s.v. *ging*, sb. senses 2, 3c). The minor humiliation undergone by Arthur in not being recognized is thus tacitly presented as deserved. It is the appropriate outcome of his youthful behavior, his *child-gered* mannerism. And this behavior in turn is a manifestation of the youthfulness of the court itself, which was earlier described as being in its "first age." The ironic reversal of this detail of the opening description is fully accomplished when the Green Knight, scoffing at the idea of meeting any one of them in single combat, says "Hit arn aboute on þis bench bot berdleȝ chylder" (280). . . .

The narrator of *Gawain*, we may safely say, is richly conscious of the disparity between the reputation for valor and warlike prowess of Arthur's knights and what actually takes place when the Green Knight thrusts himself upon them. But this does not imply that his attitude toward them involves either hostility or contempt. Because he has avoided emphasis on material luxury and worldly power in his depiction of the life of the court, the Challenge Episode is not seen as a rebuke to arrogance or sensual self-indulgence. Arthur and his knights are charmingly youthful and joyous; their pleasures are innocent. And although it is over-shadowed by the more conspicuous presence of the Green Knight, Gawain's behavior is exquisitely courteous. His self-possession in requesting that the adventure be allotted to him and in actually dealing the blow indicates clearly that he, at least, had refrained from speaking "for cortaysye" (247) rather than out of fear.

*   *   *

The above-discussed features of style manifest themselves in the poem as what might be called the characteristic mode of imagination of the narrating "I," who is here also the narrating "eye." In general, the narrator of *Gawain* tends to imagine agents and objects as they assume particular relationships within a limited space (and in limited time). He tends also to adopt the point of view of the character central in a given narrative passage as that character responds to the circumstances of the action. The result is vividness, but it is vividness of a special kind. When it is visual, it depends as much on the exact appropriateness of what is seen, by whom, and from where, as on the color, texture, or other intrinsic sensory or aesthetic qualities of the object. It is the vividness of the frozen stream that "henged heȝe ouer [Gawain's] hede in hard ysse-ikkles" (732), rather than of those streams that "thro' wavering lights and shadows broke, / Rolling a slumbrous sheet of foam below" in the landscape of "The Lotos-Eaters." In recognizing the dramatic implications of the successive details of the narrative, the reader is pulled in imagination into the world of the poem, and experiences it as a reality.

In the Challenge episode, as later in the poem, the narrator's attitude toward the hero is one of affection. And in this episode Gawain shows himself superior to the rest of the court (the king excepted) in his response to an unfamiliar, trying, and seemingly dangerous situation. As a result of this response, he is to be singled out for sore trials of chastity, of courtesy, and finally of courage. In the first there is no real question of failure. The second, conducted concomitantly by the lady in the bedchamber scenes, is the more subtle, the more suspenseful, and the more amusing of the two, though the hero's courtesy, like his chastity, is successfully maintained throughout. It is in the third that, showing himself less hero than human, he falls short, and as a result, abandons courtesy too for a few moments in an acrimonious outburst of antifeminism. In the account of these trials, as in that of the Challenge episode, the elements of discomfort, frustration, and annoyance inherent in each situation will be realized to the full, and the extent to which Gawain falls short of the ideal, by implication, clearly defined. But through it all, the narrator's time-honored atti-

tudes of solemnity and deference—mixed with a genuinely felt affection—will be maintained.

This story and the way it is told—the "what" and the "how" of the
narration—must, for the purposes of a study of style, be considered as
two different things. The historical study of style reveals that in *Sir
Gawain and the Green Knight,* the verbal expression of the story is
thoroughly traditional, to an extent that is more and more fully apparent as one becomes more familiar with the other extant works
belonging to the same tradition. But in *Gawain* the traditional features
of style do not serve the traditional purposes. They become devices for
the production of an effect in which the narrator—the presiding,
interpreting "I," with his emotions and attitudes, his manner, and
his particular mode of imaginative perception—is all-important. In
the last analysis what this narrator has to tell and the way in which he
chooses to tell it are one.

Ideals of Knighthood in
Late-Fourteenth-Century England

by Gervase Mathew

Two virtues above all were held to mark the good knight and bring him honor. They were prowess and loyalty. Prowess would seem to imply an acquired habit of skill at arms and two natural qualities, indomitability and rashness, 'Magnanimitas' and 'Audacia.' In *Gawayne* fearlessness is illustrated most often by indomitability. It is 'Audacia' that is emphasized by the Chandos Herald. He writes of Sir Ralph Hastings that he did not value death at two cherries and of Sir William Felton that he threw himself among the enemy like a man without sense and without counsel. 'Outrageus,' rash, is used as a term of praise. The same emphasis can be found in most fourteenth-century metrical romances; in *Amys and Amiloun* where Amiloun fights as if 'wode' and in the battle scenes in *Rowlande and Otuel* and in *William of Palerne*; the glory of Sir Degrevant is his 'Audacia.' The skill at arms that was presupposed was commonly illustrated by good swordsmanship and was held to be governed by a code of fair fighting. For the Chandos Herald it is the possession of prowess which merits the term 'bon chivaler' or 'chivalerous.' [1]

The sense given to 'loiautee,' loyalty, at this period is more intricate and more significant. It is a quality of the soul; 'Ot coer loiall' is a recurrent phrase in the Chandos Herald and his redactor, just as a

"Ideals of Knighthood in Late-Fourteenth-Century England" by Gervase Mathew. From Studies in Medieval History Presented to Frederick Maurice Powicke, *eds. R. W. Hunt, W. A. Pantin, and R. W. Southern (Oxford: Clarendon Press, 1948), pp. 358–62. Copyright 1948 by the Clarendon Press. Reprinted by permission of the publisher. Most of the extensive documentation of the original article has been omitted.*

[1] Worcester College Library, MS. 1; *The Life of the Black Prince by the Herald of Sir John Chandos,* ed. M. K. Pope and E. C. Lodge (Oxford, 1910).

contemporary allegorist saw all right living guarded by the keep of 'Loial Coer.' It implied fidelity to the pledged word, or loyalty to an individual owing to a transient relationship such as that of guest and host in the case of Gawayne, or loyalty to an individual because of love or friendship, 'amur' or 'amistie,' at a time when love was conventionally phrased in terms of friendship and friendship in terms of love. In the first case it was held to last until the pledge had been fulfilled; in the second until the mutual relationship which had given rise to it had ended. In the third it was ideally held to be irrevocable and of its nature incapable of change. The conflict between such loyalties or their testing was to provide both the psychological tension and the plot of most fourteenth-century romances. Through such plots it is easy to trace the steady weakening of the sense of the family unit and of the old emphasis on the bond between man and lord. But it is probable that the idea of loyalty narrowly and personally conceived had retained a strength of emotional appeal which enabled the audience of a romance to sympathize with the dilemmas of its heroes. Sir Gawayne searches the wilderness for the Green Knight that he may offer himself to be beheaded rather than break knighthood by breaking troth. Sir Amadas is persuaded by his wife to cut her and their child in two in order to fulfil a pledge, just as Arviragus would prefer that the wife he loved should commit adultery rather than break her word. Amiloun chooses leprosy and poverty rather than desert Amis in an unjust quarrel. Amis kills his two small sons in order to heal his friend.

In practice, as in the fantastic situations of romances, such a conception of honor could be a supplement to conventional Christian morality, at times strengthening and at times superseding it. Perhaps in the same fashion personal loyalty thus conceived could either strengthen or supersede the ties of a bastard feudalism. For personal friendship in itself was conceived as an alliance:

> To hold to gider at eueri nede
> In word in werk in wille in dede.

Like friendship 'Pitie' could provide the course or the excuse for direct political action. The Chandos Herald notes that the prince undertook the Spanish campaign 'pur pitie' and 'pur amistie.' For 'Pitie' seems essentially a compassion for an individual which finds expression in immediate action. John Gower could write that 'Pites la doulce et debonnaire' has Mercy for her secretary, and the Chandos Herald that the prince found his pleasure in giving aid to him who asked it on plea of suffering. The epithet had survived into the late Middle Ages from the primitive conception of the hero of the *chanson de geste* as a 'Justicier,' a punisher of wrong-doers; it remained linked with it. To John Gower the function of the true knight is to give battle against injustices. To the author of *Piers Plowman* an essential note of true knighthood is to put down wrong-doers—not a magistracy but a substitute or supplement for magistracy. The Chandos Herald emphasizes the prince's determination 'en tenir justice et droiture' 'et pur droiture sustener.' The exact meaning of 'justice' and 'droiture' in such contexts is yet to be determined; it may be suggested that though it includes both written law and custom it primarily refers to natural equity.

Three other qualities are persistently inculcated, 'largesse,' 'franchise,' and 'cortaysie.' 'Largesse' is a prodigal generosity. It is perhaps primarily valued because of the detachment from possession and the disregard for wealth that it implies. The Chandos Herald illustrates it by the 'beals dons' given by the prince, the gold and silver and rich jewels, and by 400 men that he entertained daily at his table at Bordeaux. Its moral is suggested by the statement in the *Livre des faicts* that it is a notorious thing that the good knight must be without the desire to amass treasure and riches. No epithet is more closely illustrated in fourteenth-century romances or had passed through so many evolutions since the *chansons de geste*.

By this period Franchise would seem to have taken the place of the 'debonneirete' of the early *romans courtois*. In the *Romaunt of the Rose* it had been the arrow winged by Courtesy and Courage. It remained the mark of the well bred, 'the frely fode,' it implied a certain freedom and naturalness in manner and form of approach. For the Chandos Herald it was perhaps an example of the prince's 'fraunchyse' that on meeting his wife and his son Edward during his triumphal entry into Bordeaux he dismounted and walked into the city holding their hands. Franchise was the antithesis of 'wrecced Churlishness' as in the *Frankleyn's Tale*. A form of generosity of spirit, it was close linked with fellowship as in *Gawayne*. It was controlled by courtesy.

The sense of *courtoisie* had been slowly narrowing; now it primarily meant good manners, whether in action as in the 'cortaysie' books, or in the 'techeles termes of talkyng noble' as in *Gawayne*. It

still retained some of its earlier moral implications through its association with the 'coer gentil' and with 'Bel Accueil.' On this reading
the Chandos Herald is recording examples of the prince's *courtoisie*
when he relates that he attempted to do squire's service to the captive
king of France and that he thanked his own knights 'moult humble-
ment' and that he would say to his household 'Fair sweet lords you
are more than 100 times welcome'; just as it is Gawayne's cortaysie
that leads him to thank in turn the servants of his host.

A class attitude towards woman was inextricably involved with
such good manners. Its character reflected the thirteenth-century
adage 'Gawayn was a perfect knight, he went on foot, the lady rode.'
It was expected to find expression in acts of service and its primary
object in 'dames et demoiselles de noble lignee.' But often as in the
Lyfe of Ipomydon and in *Gawayne and the Grene Knight* such
'druerie' is deliberately contrasted with love. It was the fashion
throughout the knightly class to portray marriage in terms of love
service and of *amour courtois*. In fiction romantic love was very rarely
associated with adultery. It was conceived to be the stimulus of
achievement. It was held to be irrevocable and unique.

Accomplishments and physical beauty and a power of vivid sense-
perception were highly valued. Even the heroes of metrical romances
are on occasion lettered. The capacity of listening to fine books is
admired. 'Sage' or 'Sachant' is a term of praise and even seems included in the collective noun 'Preudhomye.' Yet the ideals of knighthood remained a simple individualist code of ethics in which honor
and dishonor had the sharp contrasts of heraldic colors—like the
blood upon the snow in *Gawayne*. Some of its quality seems best
conveyed by the delight in clear bright colors and fine stuffs which
marks the literary sources for it; the gold, azure, silver, gules, and
sable, the fine silk and sendal of the Chandos Herald or the violet
and azure in the story of Sir Degrevant and the jewels of Melydor.
Some of its individualism could be suggested by that other note of
this group of metrical romances, the perpetual sense of the forest,
the absence of horizon. For it is a system of ethics which seems to pre-
suppose a class society in which personal relationships hold primary
importance and in which the emotional content is provided by a
romantic, perhaps rather adolescent, conception of personal loyalty,
friendship, and adventure.

Yet even if such ideals formed an essential part in the education of
most members of the knightly class in late-fourteenth-century Eng-

land, it is not possible to tell how far they remained accepted by them. In the new court at Eltham or at Sheen such standards may at times have seemed as naïve and as remote as the bourgeois romances parodied in *Sir Topas*. By 1390 the ideals in the Chandos Herald poem or in *Sir Gawayne* or in *Sir Degrevant* were perhaps consciously old-fashioned. They were even becoming a little insular. The French influences with which they were linked were no longer dominant among the Valois patrons with their taste for delicate sensibility, tenderness, and irony and the savor of good letters. It is Chaucer, not the author of *Sir Gawayne*, who could have been appreciated in contemporary Paris. But in England the new court culture was to vanish, perhaps in Henry of Derby it had produced its own grave-digger. The ideals of knighthood were to survive past Malory, fluctuating, modified, at last formalized in a code of honor.

Gawain: His Reputation, His Courtesy, and His Appearance in Chaucer's *Squire's Tale*

by B. J. Whiting

Gawain's relations with women are sometimes held to have had a profound effect on his general reputation.[1] One school of thought considers him originally a model of chastity and therefore ineligible for any pattern of life fixed by the rules of courtly love. Gawain's character, well-known and fixed, would not permit him to take part in an illicit affair; courtly love presupposed extra-marital relations; the current craze was for courtly love, and therefore Gawain must be supplanted by a new hero.[2] Against this theory, which is not unattractive, it must be urged, first, that the evidence for Gawain's chastity is extremely slight, and second, that Gawain's affairs are most frequent in romances tinged by courtly love. Certain it is, however, that Gawain is not a courtly lover. He is ordinarily too polite and too considerate to be described as animalistic, but he almost never becomes emotionally involved. No one ever found Gawain bewailing to the trees or stars the indifference or cruelty of a lady fair. He is never enmeshed in a long drawn out passion, nor, unlike Arthur, Lancelot

---

"Gawain: His Reputation, His Courtesy, and His Appearance in Chaucer's Squire's Tale" by B. J. Whiting. From Mediaeval Studies, *Vol. IX (Toronto: Pontifical Institute of Mediaeval Studies, 1947), pp. 203, 206, 215, 225–28. Copyright 1947 by the Pontifical Institute of Mediaeval Studies. Reprinted by permission of the publisher.*

[1] [These excerpts from a study of the traditional figure of Gawain throw an interesting light on the courtesy and chastity of the hero of *Sir Gawain and the Green Knight*. The detailed documentation of the original article has been omitted, and translations have been supplied. Ed.]

[2] Even in the late *Sir Gawain and the Green Knight*, Gawain is characterized not by chastity, but by a continence induced by his sense of social and personal obligation. The test is not of Gawain's chastity, but of his honor, and in Gawain's case, as in medieval romance generally, the two virtues are distinct.

and Tristram (twice), is he ever guilty of adultery. The most courteous of knights, he is a foil to the courtly lover through elasticity rather than chastity.

Miss Weston and others have argued that Gawain's apparent promiscuity is largely due to the failure of the writers of romance to understand his pre-history. Since Gawain's original mistress was a fairy, queen of the other world, and nameless, it was easy for her to turn up again and again under different names or without a name. Fairy mistresses and other-world brides were so prevalent, so much a part of the machinery of medieval romance, that it would be strange indeed if Gawain did not have one or more. To use that fact to regularize Gawain's *liaisons* is, at best, a debatable procedure, and illustrates one of the hazards of applying the methods of human biography to a creature of fiction. While the alleged paucity of Gawain's offspring is of some biological interest, its evidence for the number of his mistresses is slight. It is significant that though Gawain often marries, we never read of his married life or of his wives, once the marriage has been consummated. To sum up, in the romances, prose as well as verse, Gawain is the casual, good-natured and well-mannered wooer of almost any available girl. If she acquiesces, good; if not, there is sure to be another pavilion or castle not far ahead. Rarely indeed do the authors pass a moral judgment on the hero's conduct.

*   *   *

That Gawain was conspicuously lacking in the qualities demanded of the winner of the Grail will be admitted by his most ardent admirers, except perhaps those who know him only in *Sir Gawain and the Green Knight*. At his very best he is a man of war and women, one whose character requires no shading to make him the antithesis of Galahad. We are not surprised, then, that Gawain does not achieve the Grail, or even that Perceval, Bors and Lancelot go farther along the road. But he does make more progress than do most of the seekers, and we feel that he would have made still more, had it not been for a fault which would have occurred only to the religious authors of the books about the Grail. Without being entirely irreligious, Gawain is represented as lacking true contrition and a sense of the immediacy of soul's salvation. On two occasions, at least, he might have redeemed himself, but each time he evaded the opportunity with a frivolous excuse.

*   *   *

There are three distinct but interwoven causes for Gawain's loss of reputation. First is the tendency for the hero or heroes of a developing saga to become passive or tarnished. We can see this process, sometimes called epic degeneration, operating on Arthur, Charlemagne and Robin Hood, as well as on Gawain. Indeed, Gawain himself had risen to prominence as a young hero who took over some of his uncle's more active functions. Then other young heroes assumed the leading rôles in individual episodes and finally one particular new knight, Lancelot, moved into Gawain's place as Arthur's lieutenant. Second is the cult of courtly love. Gawain as a lover followed a well-defined pattern: when he met an unattached girl he made love to her; if she rebuffed him he departed; if, as more often, she welcomed his attentions, he also departed, but not as soon. With him, too, out of sight was out of mind. For him a love affair was an exchange of verbal and physical courtesies, and he had no realization of his own unworthiness or the lady's supreme condescension in granting him her slightest favor. If we also remember that, for whatever reason, he did not make love to married women, we understand that Gawain could not be a participant in any game of love played by the rules of the code. The two leading exponents of adulterous love, though not equals in courtly love, were Lancelot and Tristram, and it was natural that on this score Gawain should be subordinated to them. Third is the Grail. To achieve the Grail required consecration, chastity, spirituality and what for want of a better term may be called discriminating pacificism. Gawain had none of these qualities and was used, in some degree unjustly, to illustrate their opposites. No writer was moved to give Gawain the benefit of the pious sophistry which enabled Lancelot to come closer to the Grail than his previous conduct had warranted. When there is added to these three impersonal forces the deliberate effort of two men of letters, the author of the prose *Tristan* and Tennyson, to make Gawain a deliberate villain, we may perhaps marvel that the hero comes through the centuries as well as he does. With all the evidence in hand, and making allowances where allowances can fairly be made, Gawain remains the most distinguished and the most human of Arthur's knights.

*   *   *

A fairy at Gawain's birth promises him beauty, courtesy and honorable estate. He is called the most courteous knight of Arthur's court, or, indeed, of all the world. Courteous often has the force of a

fixed epithet, so that "le cortois" becomes almost as much a part of
his name as Mesire. There are few things which Gawain cannot do
courteously if he sets himself to it. In *Epée,* when about to go out on
an adventure, "cortoisement s'aparella" (p. 8, l. 37), and in *Carle:*

> Gawaine hent the hammer in his hand.
> & curteouslye on the gates dange.

(p. 282, ll. 133–4)

In the latter poem courtesy pays off handsomely. Despite great provo-
cation Gawain is consistently polite and deferential to his rude and
violent host. As a final reward for exquisite manners the Carl turns
his daughter over to Gawain for the night:

> saith, "Gawaine, now for thy curtesye,
> gett thee to bedd to this ffaire Lady" . . .

(p. 289, ll. 353–4)

Naturally enough, it is in his relations with ladies that Gawain's
courtesy flashes most brightly and, often, has the most pleasing results.
Courteous himself, he demands the same quality in a girl:

> Car pucele doit courtoise estre,
> sage et plaisanz et de simple estre
> et de tout bon affaitement.

[For a maiden must be courteous, well-conducted and pleasant and
guileless, and be very well brought up.]

His approach is marked by courtesy; in *Epée,* for example, he talks
with a maiden:

> Tant l'ot cortoisement parler
> Et tant lo voit de bones mors,
> Que ele l'amast par amors,
> S'ele descovrir li osast.

(p. 14, ll. 314–17)

[She heard him speak so courteously, and saw him to have such good
manners, that she would have loved him with passion, if she had dared
to reveal it.]

Because of Gawain's reputation as a lover he is the secret passion of
many maidens who have never seen him in the flesh, and as such is
the medieval prototype of some of our own cherished heroes of radio
and film. A few examples will show that there was an active Gawain

Club among the young ladies of romance. In Pseudo-Wauchier he meets a damsel whom he addresses as "dame," but at once, with the smoothness of what appears long usage, he alters his salutation to "pucele." The poet makes the approving comment, "Cortoisement et biau li dist" (III, 103, l. 12044). The damsel is impressed and, although the knight is unidentifiable in his armor, something leads her to talk about Gawain:

> Sire, bien a .ii. ans passés,
> Si com je quic, et plus assés,
> C'oï primes de lui parler,
> Et si grans biens de lui conter
> Qu'en lui a plus sens et proèce,
> Biauté, cortoisie et largèce,
> Qu'il n'an en chevalier vivant.

(III, 104, ll. 12063–69)

[Sir, full two years have passed, as I believe, and more, since I first heard talk of him, and great good I heard told of him, that there is in him more judgment and prowess, handsomeness, courtesy, and generosity, than there is in any living knight.]

She is too polite to dwell long on an absent ideal:

> "Dont vos pri-jou par cortoisie
> Que vos nommés." "Ma douce amie,
> J'ai nom Gauwain."

(ll. 12075–77)

["So I ask you, for courtesy, that you tell your name." "My sweet friend, my name is Gawain."]

At first she does not believe it, not apparently so much doubting his word as her own luck. She has once seen a portrait of Gawain, and feels certain that she would recognize

> Ses bones teces, ses bontés,
> Ses courtoisies, ses biautés.

(III, 105, ll. 12103–4)

[His good points, his excellences, his courtesies, his good looks.]

Will the stranger be so kind as to disarm and let her see if he is really and truly Gawain? He will, he does, and he is. Their acquaintance grows by leaps and bounds:

Par .i. baisier l'en a saisie;
D'amours, de droit, de cortoisie,
Ont plus ensamble tant parlé
Et boinement ris et jué
Qu'elle a pierdu nom de pucele:
Sel nomme amie et damosele.

(III, 106, ll. 12127–32)

[With a kiss he has captured her; of love, of right, of courtesy, they have
talked together so much more, and lustily laughed and played, that she
has lost her name of maiden, and so become "love" and "lady".]

Soon after Gawain leaves—since he is on a quest he cannot linger—
the young lady's father rides up, and she is so indiscreet as to inform
him that she has lost her virginity to Gawain, omitting any mention,
however, of her own enthusiastic complicity. Ensuing events are
fatal to the father and damaging to her brother. She herself, as it
turns out, is pregnant, but Gawain escapes with his courtesy. . . .

*   *   *

[There is] a passage in *Perlesvaus*, where some girls had refused to
credit his identity because he had gone to sleep when they offered him
their services:

se ce fust cil Gavains qui niés est le roi Artu, il parlast a nos autrement,
e trovissions en lui plus de deduit que en cestui; mes cist est uns Gavains
contrefez (I, 95, ll. 1814–6).

[if this were the Gawain who is the nephew of King Arthur, he would
have spoken to us differently, and we would have found in him more
pleasure than in this one; but this is a counterfeit Gawain.]

Sir Gawain and the Green Knight

by John Speirs

Sir Gawain and the Green Knight is a great English poem. It has
not so much been simply neglected as it has suffered the wrong kind
of attention, the kind of attention that has perpetuated its essential
neglect as a poem. For it would, indeed, be hard to say what in the
nature of the poem itself exactly it is that has ever been attended to.
The attention has not been a literary-critical attention, the attention
that is appropriate to a poem. It has been of the kind that has tended
to obscure rather than to expose the poem itself, a directing of attention away from the poem towards extrinsic matters, an interposition
of pedantic irrelevances between the poem and the reader, an elaborate evasion of its significance. The poem has never been attended to
as what in itself it uniquely is.

The mere mechanics of deciphering the text are, it may be admitted, troublesome. That is not simply because its language is a
dialect of English (that of the North West Midlands) which is not
the dialect which became our English; it is because (to speak out
bluntly) of the unintelligent way in which the poem has been edited.
The edition at present used by students and on which they are examined (it is, of course, the *edition* rather than the *poem* they are
examined on) merely slavishly reproduces the deficiencies, confusions
and inconsistencies of the copyist's spelling in the Cotton Nero IX
MS. That kind of thing could have been done better by making
photostat copies of the MS. itself for the university libraries. The
introduction and lengthy, mostly irrelevant notes, which further over-
lay the poem in this edition (as in most other editions of so-called
Middle English texts), illustrate again the depressing 'scholarly' technique of interposing extrinsic 'points of interest' between the reader

"Sir Gawain and the Green Knight" by *John Speirs. From* Scrutiny, *XVI (1949)*,
*274–90. Copyright 1949 by the Syndics of Cambridge University Press. Reprinted by
permission of the author and the publisher.*

and the poem and so distracting attention from the poem itself to these interposed obstacles; as if the significance of a great poem were not in itself the most difficult thing in the world to grasp without the deliberate obtrusion and exaggeration of external 'difficulties.' It seems the editors were themselves unaware of the significance and value of the poem they were editing. It is time the universities looked a little into the kind of thing they are responsible for.[1]

What little show of criticism of the poem there has been seems to have been governed by the determination to relate it to the mediæval French romances. It is certainly a part of the function of criticism to see a poem in its place in relation to other poems. Seeing the poem as what in itself it is will indeed be simultaneous with seeing it in the place it establishes for itself in the order which all poems (it may be agreed) establish in relation to each other. The place of *Sir Gawain and the Green Knight*—and *because* it is a great poem it is a central place—is in the English tradition. It belongs to the first great creative moment of (I shall dare to say) *modern* English literature— the moment of the *Canterbury Tales* and of *Piers Plowman*. These three English poems, though robustly independent from each other, are not accidentally contemporary. Their very unlikeness to each other is a guarantee of the integrity, the individuality, the uniqueness of each. They are each different, as Ben Jonson is different from Shakespeare. But they have the same kind of relation to each other —and indeed to Shakespeare and to Ben Jonson—as Ben Jonson has to Shakespeare. When the important regional differences have been allowed for, they remain English poems; they have in common what is, as a whole, the same English community; they are nourished (allowing fully for their regional differences) by a common English soil. For *Sir Gawain and the Green Knight* is the crown, the masterpiece of a whole school of poetry—the alliterative poetry of the North West of England—contemporary with Chaucer and Langland, distinct from either, but equally an important, though less recognized, element in the English tradition. I refer not only to the poems which appear in the same MS. with *Sir Gawain and the Green Knight*— *Cleanness, Patience* and *The Pearl* [2]—but also to such poems as the

---

[1] The old E.E.T.S. edition which has been supplanted by Tolkien and Gordon's remains much the better edition to read the poem in, if only it were made generally available.

[2] To suppose as a matter of course or probability that because these poems appear in the same MS and dialect they are—on these grounds alone—by the same author

alliterative *Morte Arthure, The Aunters of Arthure at the Tarn Wadling* and *The Destruction of Troy.*

There is no use my ignoring my feeling that the 'scholarly' concern to derive this superb English poem from French romances (even if the very existence of these has to be hypothetical), while allowing that somehow it goes one better than they do, has been such as, in effect, insidiously to belittle it. By establishing the 'derivativeness' of any given poem, or the limiting 'conditions' within which it had to be composed, it becomes more easy safely to do it down, to ignore its uniqueness, what it does that no other poem does. To attend to an assortment of French romances and Celtic tales is not at all the same thing as to attend to *Sir Gawain and the Green Knight*; just as to attend to Holinshed's Chronicle is not at all the same thing as to attend to *Macbeth.* To summarize the 'plots' of these French romances and of *Sir Gawain and the Green Knight* and to attend to and compare these summaries is still less the same thing as to attend to and compare the poems themselves. Such methods are a short cut to nowhere; they are not the methods of literary criticism. Yet to suppose that a task of critical elucidation and value has been accomplished by such comparisons of summaries is a form of self deception that has been exceptionally prevalent among literary scholars discussing mediæval texts.

There is no need to deny that the author of *Sir Gawain and the Green Knight* may have had a French romance before him, just as Shakespeare has *his* 'sources.' It is unlikely that he did *not* read (or listen to) French romances. But even if we establish that a French romance (or group of romances) was the poem's *literary* source, we have got no nearer the poem itself. The poem is clearly not *just* a courtly romance, and it is totally a very different kind of thing from a French romance. Yet the sheer unlikeness of the English alliterative poem to all the French romances we have has not discouraged the attachment of apparently supreme importance to the relating of it to 'French Romance.' It is as if the placing of some of Shakespeare's plays

---

is quite uncritical. Yet that is what the scholars who make a property of Middle English literature—detaching it from the rest of English literature for the purpose —do not hesitate to do. It is another instance of the uselessness of scholarship which is unqualified by a literary training and sensibility and unguided by a literary-critical discipline. What can be said is that in this particular locality there was a whole school of poetry; and that that poetry is such that it implies a cultivated society.

in the context of the 'Italian Novel' were to be regarded as the function of Shakespearean criticism. The particular French romances which are not there for *Sir Gawain and the Green Knight* to be derived from are lightheartedly assumed to have been there and to have been lost.[3] These hypothetical romances are discussed in relation to the poem almost as if they, rather than it, had a real existence.

Our task is to see the object, the English poem as what it positively is, and that is not, of course, the abstracted 'story.' If the value were in the 'story' in itself, then our editors' summary of it in the forefront of their edition would be all that we should require to read. It is what is made of the 'story,' how it is realized, the kind of significance it is made to bear, what the poem totally communicates or does that is our object. To judge from the abstracted 'story' Morgan le Fay is the *cause* of all the events. Yet in the poem itself she is not at all felt to account for these events.[4] To do so she would have had to be realized as Lady Macbeth is realized. Her envy of Guinevere would have had to be as real a force, present in the texture of the poem, as the Macbeths' ambition. But it is not. The old woman of the Second Fit of the poem *is* realized, and at the end of the whole poem Gawain is told that she was Morgan. But where the old woman occurs the point is not that she is Morgan, but simply that she is an old woman. What the significance of the old woman is, in contrast to the young woman, will, of course, have to be considered in any critical analysis of the poem. The 'explanation'—Morgan's envy of Guinevere —introduced rather perfunctorily at the end of the poem (from the literary source or 'authority,' perhaps) is, in effect, no more than a bone for the rationalizing mind to play with and be kept quiet with.

Yet though we may dismiss the abstracted 'story' as of no value in itself, we may well ask how it is that this particular rendering of the 'story' (or combination of 'stories') has turned out to be a great unified work of art. For the English poem has the unity of a very completed, very deliberately constructed and finished work of art. But not just constructed. The unity is more than a construction; it has the character of an organic unity, a unity of growth. A conscious and deliberate artist (bearing, perhaps, the same kind of relation to his subject

---

[3] One of the curiosities of Tolkien and Gordon's introduction is a diagram in which letters of the alphabet represent French originals that do not exist but are assumed to have existed. It is one of the things which candidates for the London English Honours B.A. annually memorise.

[4] *Pace* Tolkien and Gordon's Introduction, p. xi.

matter as we imagine Homer does) the poet has constructed. But in so doing he has, as it were, co-operated with some inner organizing, unifying and realizing principle of life and growth. The result is both a satisfying surface completeness and a full-bodied, matured completion or fulfilment. We may perhaps legitimately begin by inquiring generally what this principle of life might be that has activated the genius of the poet and made the poem the remarkable Shakespearean unity it is, though only an analysis of the poem itself can more exactly define its nature.

It is a case in which the literary critic may appropriately find his initial hint in some of the observations of the anthropologists, provided he recognizes that that does not relieve him from his own responsibility and function of literary criticism, criticism of the particular poem as in itself it in fact is. Miss J. L. Weston's *From Ritual to Romance* and *The Quest of the Grail*—to a lesser extent the chapters on the Folk Drama in E. K. Chambers's *Mediæval Stage*—provide exactly the hint we may have been looking for. Our poem is clearly a midwinter festival poem. The seasonal theme (as any detailed analysis of the poem will bear out) is the poem's underlying, indeed pervasive theme.

The Green Knight whose head is chopped off at his own request and who is yet as miraculously or magically alive as ever, bears an unmistakable relation to the Green Man—the Jack in the Green[5] or the Wild Man of the village festivals of England and Europe. He *is* in fact no other than a recrudescence in poetry of the Green Man. Who the Green Man is is well established. He is the descendent of the Vegetation or Nature god of (whatever his local name) almost universal and immemorial tradition whose death and resurrection mythologizes the annual death and re-birth of nature—in the East the dry and rainy seasons, in Europe winter and spring. The episode (the First Fit of our poem) in which the Green Knight rides into the hall of Arthur's castle among the courtly company at the Christmas feast and demands to have his head chopped off is exactly a Christmas pageant play or interlude—a castle version of the village Folk Play—become real. The central episode of the traditional Folk Play, Sword Dance and Morris Dance was (as Chambers shows) a

---

[5] Represented by the lad wreathed in hawthorn, a walking bush, in the May Day village festivals. The leafy screens carried by the restoration army in *Macbeth*, Birnam Wood advancing on Macbeth's castle, have certainly a related symbolic significance.

mock beheading or slaying followed by a revival or restoration to life
(often by the Doctor who administered to the corpse the contents of
an outsize bottle—the elixir of life).

A recently published book by C. J. P. Cave, *Roof Bosses in
Mediæval Churches*, has come very conveniently to hand to demon-
strate the vitality of the Green Man in mediæval England. Mr.
Cave's photography has revealed very distinctly carvings on the roofs
of cathedrals and parish churches which could previously only be
distinguished through field glasses, or in some cases, because in
shadow, have never been seen till this day. Ecclesiastics walking down
below could not have seen what the carver was doing up there (60
or 70 feet up); he could carve what he liked. What he did carve again
and again (as Mr. Cave's photographs wonderfully reveal) was a face
with leaves sprouting from the corners of its mouth, its eye-lids, eye-
brows and ears, the face of the Green Man.[6]

The other protagonist, the Sir Gawain of our poem, is correspond-
ingly related to a traditional Gawain who (Miss Weston tells us)
did not originally belong among Arthur's knights any more than
does the Green Knight. Gawain's traditional rôle (she convincingly
establishes) was that of the hero, the agent who brought back the
spring, restored the frozen life-processes, revived the god—or (in
later versions) cured the king. Though there is no mention of that
in our poem, there are other poems in which Sir Gawain is mysteri-
ously spoken of as having the skill of a healer or doctor—not one of
the usual skills of courtly knighthood.

The winter landscape through which, in our poem, Sir Gawain
rides on his quest for the Green Chapel, where on New Year's Day
he is to renew his acquaintance with the Green Knight, is again the
northern European Waste Land, the land that has been (not, as in
the east, dried up) frozen up. If it is (implicitly) 'enchantment' which
the land suffers from in our poem, it is the kind it suffers from every
winter in the north of Europe; it is frozen up.

There are some unexpected underground resemblances (which
may be glanced at here in transition) between Sir Gawain and Piers.
Piers the Plowman—in one part of Langland's poem described as
'the leche of life' and associated with the seasonal cycle—is identified

---

[6] It can scarcely be accidental that so many village pubs in England are called
The Green Man.

with Christ, and Christ is the hero who (in Passus XVIII) harrows
Hell, releases imprisoned life, restores the dead,

Lord of life and of light.

It is the Easter theme; the dreamer, appropriately, awakes to the
sound of the Easter bells. The episode has *its* dramatic counterpart,
too, the Harrowing of Hell of the Miracle Plays.

Sir Gawain and the Green Knight is of course, near the surface, a
Christian poem. But it is Christian rather as some of the mediæval
Christmas carols are Christian, as Christmas itself is Christian; Christian in harmony with pre-Christian nature belief and ritual, a Christian re-interpretation of these. It is Christian to about the same depth
as it is a courtly romance. The value of 'courtesy'—Sir Gawain is
among other things the pattern of courtesy, the most courteous of
Arthur's courtly company—is certainly one of the values defined in
the poem and brought out in relation to the other values in their
order, Christian and pre-Christian; and these other values are pre-
courtly.

The fundamental feeling or *knowledge* in the poem, the hidden
source which the poet has tapped, the ultimate source of the poem's
actuality, strength and coherence, is the knowledge, which the age-
old experience of the race has turned into an assured knowledge,
that there is life inexhaustible at the roots of the world even in the
dead season, that there is perpetually to be expected the unexpected
spring re-birth. The whole poem is, in its very texture—its imagery
and rhythm—an assertion of belief in *life* as contrasted with winter
deprivation and death; and it seems finally to discover, within the
antagonism between man and nature, between the human and the
other-than-human, an internal harmony, even a kind of humorous
understanding.

There might be no great impropriety in describing as Elizabethan
the poem's completeness of delighted acceptance and vivid consciousness of profane life as that takes the senses in rich color and decorative pattern, in costly magnificence of costume and tapestry, jewellery
and embroidery, in elaborate and subtle craftsmanship in metal, wood
and stone; and of life also as it expresses itself in ceremonial banqueting, pageantry, music and 'carolling' (dancing and singing in
unison) and in the strenuous physical exertions and hazards of tourneying and hunting; gay, Homeric laughter recurs throughout the

scenes in the castles. Yet the rich and exuberant imagery of the poem is strictly controlled by the inner intention; it has its symbolic value in relation to the main, the 'life' significance. The jewellery and embroidery, for example, are related to the underlying fertility theme, contrasted with the chastity theme, as the feasting and generous hospitality in the castles contrast with the winter dearth.

The poem depends for its local effects largely upon sheer weight and heaped-up pressure of language[7]—a piling-up of language that contrasts with Chaucer's civilized simplicity—masses of bright colors and concatenations of differentiated sounds. But it is not just lavishness and excess; it is all built into an art as firm as Ben Jonson's; it is even Shakespearean in the way it is all unfalteringly, unerringly controlled towards a total inclusive significance.

The poem is in four Fits. It opens at once on the note of the indestructibility and perpetual renewal of life. Arthur's castle is placed in history as one of the phoenixes of Troy, the utterly destroyed city—

> The borg brittened and brent to brondes and askes

—from which the so many new cities and kingdoms of the Western World have sprung. . . . The youthfulness of Arthur and of Arthur's folk—

> For al was this fayre folk in her first age

—introduces the theme of youth in contrast to age which is an aspect of the spring-winter (or New Year-Old Year) theme. The poem thus launched is sustained right through as a Christmas-New Year festival poem. The note of feasting—contrasted with the winter deprivation experienced by Gawain on his journey in the Second and Fourth Fits—keeps recurring. Compared with this poem's expression of the jollity, the confident belief in life of the mediæval English folk (one need not in this respect differentiate the castle folk from the village folk) much poetry since the Elizabethan sounds melancholy and weak.

Arthur looks for a marvel, Christmas being the season of marvels (what could be more marvellous than a birth in the dead season) and indeed the ceremonial banquet has hardly commenced, the first course brought in with 'crakkyng of trumpes,' when

---

[7] One of my Exeter students once counted that there are 20 different words for a man in the poem.

> Ther hales in at the halle dor an aghlich mayster.

He is no mummer disguised as a Green Knight who rides into the
hall; he *is* the Green Knight.

The huge impression—the Green Knight on the green horse—is
massively built up. He is not just faerie but robustly substantial and
a fiercely humorous character. The emphasis on his glittering array
—the jewel-like greenness of his green color and that of his horse,
the glittering green jewellery, the rich embroidery of multiplied
'bryddes and flyghes'—is unmistakably significant of life resurgent.
But more considered recognition of this significance had better be
postponed till we come to the counterpart, in the structural balance,
of the description of the Green Knight, the arming of Sir Gawain
in the Second Fit. This predilection for jewels, for example, is certainly not just the influence of the lapidaries or an interest in what
the contemporary jewellers and goldsmiths had to offer.

The 'vegetation' aspect of the Green Knight will be immediately
recognized. His green beard is like a bush, and together with his
long green hair covers his chest and back all round down to his
elbows. He carries a holly branch in one hand—

> a holyn bobbe
> That is grattest in grene when greves are bare

—and in the other a huge axe (the weapon fertility symbol). He is
as green as green verdure. It would indeed be singular not to feel
that he is an up-cropping in poetry of the old vegetation god. After
his head has been chopped off he is as vigorously alive as before, like
a pollard tree, like John Barleycorn in the old ballads against whom
came 'three kings from the West, their victory to try,' and who,
though killed and buried, 'sprang up again. And that surprised them
all.'

My own experience is that the reader instinctively feels him to be
an intruder from a pre-Christian, pre-courtly world. Something of
the old untamed, unreclaimed north of Europe has come back here
(though the Green Knight will be discovered not merely to typify
the destructive, menacing aspects of wild nature hostile to pioneer-
ing humans in their struggle to maintain their clearings in forests
and swamps). He carries no knightly arms but wields a Danish axe—
the stress is on the primitive and heathen nature of the weapon. A
'salvage' intruder, he 'breaks the good feast,' disturbs the ceremonious

courtly order with his presence and his challenge; the contrast is, at one level, between 'nature' and 'sophistication.' He evokes a half-amused, half-horrified fascination. If he is life, he is wild, uncouth, raw life. His demeanor and his behavior in this castle of courtesy are outrageously discourteous; he behaves, as if radically a 'villeyn,' with contemptuous humorous rudeness. In essence he is the *other*—the other than human. . . .

The chopping off of his own head is to this amazing fellow but a 'Crystemas gomen.' With a savage yell ('a runisch rout') he flings out of the hall, fire struck from the flints by his horse's hooves. Fire, later, is also struck from the hooves of Gawain's horse; and the flicker of fire in the *other* castle (of the Second and Third Fits) is too frequent to have an accidental significance.

The opening paragraphs of the Second Fit, superbly conveying an impression of the changing seasons, the revolving year, are not mere decoration. They are integral to the poem; they rise from the core of the unifying seasonal experience. We are not just told that a year has passed; we experience the year changing, the alternating pattern of the seasons. . . .

The Shakespearean phrases ('al rypes and rotes' . . . 'in yister-dayes mony') remind the modern reader that the language of the poem is radically the same language as Shakespeare's. The analogy with human life—human life has its seasons—an analogy familiar to us in Shakespeare underlies the melancholy note of transience. The harmony between man and nature is here a harmony in their common fate of transience. Spring and summer, though vividly re-joiced in, are episodes in the perpetual process of change. The day approaches when Gawain must set off on his quest for the Green Chapel to keep his tryst with the Green Knight there on New Year's Day and take the return blow. The concluding emphasis is on the waning of the year. The year's revolution has, however, brought round again the Christmas-New Year season. The poem is thus main-tained right through as a Christmas and New Year festival poem.

The arming of Sir Gawain, which (as already observed), corre-sponds, in the structural balance, to the description of the Green Knight, is also not mere decoration; it is not just the mediæval romancer and his castle audience's interest in knightly accoutrement, armor and weapons. The representatives of life, including the youth-ful hero whose task it is to bring back life, have always (the an-thropologists tell us) been glittering figures. The throng of dancing

youths who in the ancient rituals accompanied the god, the Maruts
of India, the Corybantes and Couretes of the Greeks, the Salii of the
Romans—the predecessors of the Sword Dancers and Morris Dancers
of more recent folk festivals—were glitteringly arrayed; in their
dances, designed to stimulate the reproductive energies of nature,
they carried flashing weapons, symbolical of fertility. In Sir Gawain's
array, and that of his horse, red color, as distinguished from the
gleaming green of his opposite, and gold—

> That al glytered and glent as glem of the sun

—predominate. There is again a profusion of jewels and a silk embroidery of birds—'papiayes' and 'tortors'—

> As mony burde theraboute had ben seven wynter.

His array thus associates Gawain also with life resurgent.

Nor is it accidental that Sir Gawain's emblem is the pentangle,
an ancient life symbol. It appears as one of the figures on the Tarot
Pack. It was believed (Miss Weston tells us) to 'give power over the
other world.' [8] The Sword Dancers, as they enclose the head in their
mock beheading, make the figure of the pentangle; as the dancers
'hold up the sign, they cry triumphantly "A nut! a nut!"' [9] In Sir
Gawain and the Green Knight, the pentangle has acquired a Christian significance; but the pre-Christian significance unmistakably underlies and is active in the poem.

The winter landscape through which Gawain now rides on his
quest for the Green Chapel is again not mere decorative background
to a romance; it is the northern European Waste Land. That is to
say, it is actual winter as it may be experienced any winter among
the mountains of North Wales after a blizzard. The geography of
Gawain's search for the Green Chapel is, and is intended to be,
significant, or why else should we be told in such detail how he left
the court in Somerset (Arthur's court representing the center of

---

[8] The significance of the pentangle (Faust's 'Druid's foot' that kept Mephisto
from crossing the threshold) is preserved in the 'Five for the symbol at your door'
of the old English counting-song Green Grow the Rushes O, where also Two is
'for the lilly-white boys clothèd all in green, O.'

[9] From Ritual to Romance, p. 93.

'Nut' means 'knot'—as in the game 'nuts in May' which means 'breast-knots or
nosegays in May'; in our poem it is said that the English call the pentangle 'the
endeles knot.'

Christian culture, civilization) to search Wales? And right through
Wales to Anglesey—the Druid country, the home of the pre-Christian
culture, the ancient religion of Britain, and where Gawain was the
favorite hero and whence the original Gawain legend came—and so
to the Wirral? After that the whereabouts of his wanderings becomes necessarily a mystery. The point is that Gawain *expected* the
Green Chapel and the Green Man to be where the cult belonged,
perhaps survived. And this specification of the real countryside of the
quest makes Gawain's subsequent wanderings in the waste full of
monsters more blood-chilling: it prevents the reader from feeling he is
merely in the stock fairy-tale world of romance and can discount the
horrors—Gawain's waste is felt to be real and perilous indeed.

The actuality of the experience of desolation—Gawain's experience
of being a stranger in a mountainous frozen region—depends upon
the actuality of this winter landscape. The experience is sharply
distinct because the landscape which is its 'objective equivalent' is
(in contrast to the indefinite dream landscapes of the *Faerie Queene*)
sharply distinct. It is a landscape from which God (originally perhaps the god) appears to have withdrawn, a landscape desolate of
humans, inhabited by un-human creatures, beasts and monsters
against which Gawain must hazard his life. The succession of tests
which Gawain will undergo has commenced. 'The test preceding and
qualifying for initiation into the secrets of physical life, consisted in
being brought into contact with the horrors of physical death.' (J. L.
Weston, *The Quest of the Grail.*) . . .

The Christian knight, remembering that it is Christmas Eve, prays
to Christ and Mary for some lodging where he might hear mass and
matins on Christmas morning. . . . As if in answer to his prayer he
is confronted with the miracle of a castle. It is an ancient experience
of the race. You are crossing a desert; you look again and (as by
magic) the desert is a garden, a paradise—as desert land may (often
does) become quite suddenly after rainfall. So here, unexpectedly, in
the Waste Land is a castle where the knight, after deprivation, will
be entertained with abundance of food and drink. The castle is unmistakably a version of the Grail Castle. (There is no mention of the
Grail in our poem; but always associated with the fleeting appear-
ances of the Grail, the life-giving vessel, are just such windfalls of
food and drink.)

In contrast to the rocks the castle seems almost fragile, as if it might
vanish again in an instant by magic.

> Chalkwhyt chymnes . . .
> That pared out of papure purely hit semed.

But it is multiplex in detail,[10] a multiplicity of towers and turrets, signifying again fertility—as innumerable stalks thrust upward from the ground in spring—and colorful as flowers are. It is islanded by water, oasis-like in effect. Gawain is here nearer than he knows to the hidden source of life.

In the structural balance of the poem this castle balances, on the one hand, the Green Chapel of the Fourth (and final) Fit—Gawain has come first not to a chapel but a castle—on the other hand, Arthur's castle. The lord of this *other* castle (Sir Bercilak de la Haut-desert—the surname is perhaps significant) will, in the Fourth Fit, turn out to be the Green Knight. Between the robust and boisterous lord of the castle, a huge man of mature age, and the Green Knight, there is a concealed resemblance, allowing that the color of his beard is now reddish brown and not green.

> Brode, brycht, was his berde, and al bever-hued.
> Felle face as the fyre . . .

His association with fire has unmistakably the same kind of significance that the fire festivals had; the flicker of fire—fire light and torch light—is (as previously remarked) characteristic of this castle. Gawain and the Green Knight of the First Fit have here in the Second Fit in some respects changed places. After he has been clothed in fresh garments[11] the youthful Gawain looks like the spring.

> The Ver by his visage veraryly hit semed
> Welnegh to uche hathel, alle on hues,
> Lowande and lufly alle his lymmes under. . . .

It is as if the spring itself has come to the castle and been welcomed. As a guest, Gawain is restored to the warmth of human hospitality before the Yule fire.

> A cheyer byfore the chemne, ther charcole brenned.

[10] The editors here interpose the red herring of 14th century castle architecture.
[11] We may compare those who have 'suffered a sea-change' in *The Tempest*.

'But the rarity of it is, which is indeed almost beyond credit . . . that our garments, being, as they were, drenched in the sea, hold notwithstanding their freshness and glosses, being rather new-dyed than stained with salt-water.'

The rebirth significance of the change of garments will be familiar enough.

As the plentiful food and drink with which—in this hostelry of the Green Man—Gawain is generously refreshed contrasts with the winter deprivation, so also the domestic comfort and sumptuousness of the interior of the castle contrasts with the inhospitable rocks. In return, Sir Gawain is to the folk in the castle the pattern of courtesy, 'the fyne fader of nurture.'

There are in the castle a young woman and an old woman. The lady hostess, Sir Bercilak's wife, is youthful and lovely. . . . She is accompanied, however, by another lady who in contrast to her is old and withered. . . . Whoever this withered ancient is in the 'story' (she is, as we happen to be told at the very end of the poem, Morgan—originally, the scholars tell us, a Celtic goddess) the point here is immediately the contrast between youth and age, which has its significance in relation to the underlying seasonal theme. Winter is the season when the year has lost its vigor, spring when the year recovers its youth; the year grows old in winter, young again in spring. The one woman is what the other turns into. Age is what youth turns into—the flesh withers. But in relation to the seasonal theme the order is here also reversible; the young woman supplants the old. The old year (in this respect there is doubtless an underground connection with the envy of Morgan) works the mischief, produces the frozen world simply by being old. Underlyingly the old woman and the young woman are the Old and the New Year.[12]

When the feast of Christmas draws to a close Gawain's host tells him he knows where the Green Chapel is—it is close at hand—and bids him rest in the castle for the three days that remain. Again there is a compact. During each of these three days the lord of the castle proposes to be abroad hunting. Each evening Gawain will exchange whatever he may have won during the day in the castle for whatever his host may have won in the chase.

The events of these three days before New Year's Day—the day of Gawain's tryst at the Green Chapel—are the subject of the Third Fit. They are days of apparent resting for Gawain but really of most perilous testing. The peril is the greater because Gawain does not know he is being tested; on the contrary, these days have been assigned to relaxation. Yet on his success or failure in these days of testing by the gay, youthful lady, his distractingly lovely hostess, will depend, though he does not guess it, his success or failure, indeed his life, at

[12] Such figures were familiar features of the annual folk festivals. The Romans had their Mamurius Veturius and his female counterpart, Anna Perenna.

the Green Chapel. Though the original, and still the underlying, purpose of the diverse tests—to find out whether or not Gawain is a fit agent to bring back the spring—is resolved into the conception of a testing of fitness for Christian knighthood, chastity has here nothing very particularly to do with monastic asceticism. Chastity has immemorially been a requirement in fertility—or nature—ceremonies and initiations. The chastity theme—chastity as a pre-condition of fertility —is here complementary to the fertility theme.

The hunts are symbolically the doing-to-death of the qualities of the natural man which Courtesy has to vanquish; the deer is timidity or cowardice, the boar ferocity, the fox animal cunning. Gawain's first natural reaction at the first entrance of the lady is to pretend to be asleep and evade the issue if he can (the deer); at her second visit she invites him to violate her forcefully (the boar); on the third occasion Gawain partially identifies himself with the cunning (the fox) of the proffer of the Green Girdle—which later in the poem he recognizes as having been a snare—by accepting and concealing it. The hunts are thus a symbolic parallel of what Gawain is doing in the castle, in the way of self-conquest, to maintain the ideal of the Christian knight— as well as realistic hunts. The poem implies an audience trained to be on the alert for a symbolic—as well as a literal—meaning; it is what made the poem possible as both sophisticated art and a popular poem. The hunts move successively to a climax which is symbolic; the boar, we should think, would follow the fox, if the crescendo were literal-dramatic and not, as it is, spiritual-symbolic.

Further, the spoils of each day's hunt both correspond, in the exchange, to the kisses of the lady and provide in midwinter the foison, the plenty that is consumed at each evening's feast; for the note of feasting continues right through the Third Fit. The Green Man now appears as the huntsman. The intimate association of vegetable and animal life, of crops and herds, has always been recognized. The three hunts of our poem underlyingly correspond to the animal sacrifices of fertility rituals; they are sacrificial hunts which provision the successive ceremonial feasts. Each hunt has its own character corresponding to the character of the creature hunted; the first day's hunt is a deer hunt, the second a boar hunt, the third a fox hunt. The poem is endlessly various, fertile in diversity of invention. . . .

The poet of *Sir Gawain and the Green Knight* was evidently a very conscious artist, conscious of what he wanted to do and of what he was doing. It seems probable that he had consciously in mind—may

have himself witnessed—the ritual the story of which underlies the
poem. This underlying ritual and the poet's belief in its value as myth
is what gives the poem its life. But it is not what has made the poem
—not simply a record of a ritual—a complex work of art. A conscious
artist, the poet *begins* from a myth; he *ends* with the poem we
have. . . .

PART TWO

View Points

Heinrich Zimmer

. . . Thus concludes the tale; but we are left with a question. Who, namely, was that weird, imperious being, qualified to challenge, test, unmask, and pass sentence? The Green Knight who could tuck his head under his arm and appear with it in place again, whose wife was the fairest temptress in the world, and whose Green Chapel was a kind of eerie crypt, "the cursedest kirk," as Gawain judged it, "that e'er I came in!"—who is he and what is his name?

In folklore and fairy tale the dead not uncommonly carry their heads under their arms to frighten the people they meet. They toss their heads up into the air and play ninepins with their skulls. Pale green, furthermore, is the color of livid corpses: the paintings of the Buddhist art of Tibet, which adhere in their color symbolism to a very definitely prescribed tradition, employ such a green to denote whatever appertains to the kingdom of King Death. We may safely assume that the death-green, towering apparition out of the forlorn valley of the "cursedest kirk," carrying an archaic ax over his shoulder instead of a contemporary, chivalric Christian sword and mounted on a steed as remarkable both for color and for size as himself, was the great reaper, Death. And the dazzlingly beautiful woman, embodying and representing the glamour of the world, offering the cup of desire, tempting to enjoy, is Life, Death's bride.

The legend of the Buddha contains a celebrated instance of this ancient and apparently universal mythological theme of the testing of the hero by the personifications of death and life. During the epochal night when the Savior was in meditation under the Bo-tree, on the Immovable Spot, and on the brink of realization, he was ap-

From The King and the Corpse, *by Heinrich Zimmer, ed. Joseph Campbell (New York: Pantheon Books, 1943), pp. 76–81. Second edition copyright © 1957 by Bollingen Foundation, New York. Bollingen Series XI. Distributed by Princeton University Press. Reprinted by permission of the publisher. The original footnotes have been omitted.*

proached by the supreme tempter Māra, "he who kills," "he who puts to death." Māra came in the guise of an attractive youth, carrying a lute; Māra's other name is Kāma, "desire," "lust." And he paraded three voluptuous damsels before the Buddha's eyes (they are termed Māra's daughters in the legend) who attempted to display themselves; but the hero was unmoved. Then the tempter, assuming his furious aspect, amassed his demon army so that—as in the temptation of Sir Gawain—the lure of life and the terror of annihilation should assault the hero simultaneously. Devils in battle gear surrounded and stormed the solitary, silent figure. And just as Gawain was tempted thrice by the woman, so was the Buddha by the three daughters; as Gawain faced the threat of the ax, so the Buddha faced the hurled missiles of the horde. The devils menaced his meditation by the very terror of their faces—many of them the visages of beasts and birds of prey. They flung burning trees, rocks, flaming mountains, but the Savior remained unmoved; for he knew that the tumult all around him, the fury of the army, and the allure of Māra's daughters represented no more than a mirror reflection of the inner, elementary forces of his own primitive human nature, which were clinging still to phenomenal existence, clamoring for carnal assuagement, and dreading the destruction of the physical frame. By the act of comprehending the terror and allure as the two manners of deportment of a single master tempter, the World Savior released himself from the cosmic enthrallment of his longing and fearing ego. Recognizing that the opposites, though contrary in apparent form, were the paired manifestations of a unique reality, he remained steadfast between. The last fitful flame of personal feeling was made extinct in him. (As "The Buddha," i.e., "The Enlightened One," he was "The Extinct One," the one who had passed into Nirvāna.) And so the damsels paraded their charms before empty eyes and the hurled missiles were transformed into flowers of adoration. The antagonist, with all his devils and daughters, had at last to withdraw.

The correspondences between these temptations of Gautama, which, according to the Buddhist tradition, represented the final step in his initiation to "The Kingly Lion Throne of the Teacher of Gods and Men," and those of Sir Gawain are obvious. In both cases death incarnate functions as the master of initiation. The champion of the Round Table fares less gloriously than Gautama, for, after all, he is not a world savior but only "the best of knights"; nevertheless, his romance is a version of the same universal mystery. Through the valley of death he is conducted to the aloof and lonely sanctuary of life renewed, and there, having withstood the trial, is reborn. This is a chivalric medieval version of the mystery of dying to the transient individuality—which is compounded of desire and fear—and gaining resurrection in the higher life immortal.

The gift bestowed on the initiate, the green girdle of the color of death—who but Death himself could have bestowed this boon? It confers immortality, releases the bearer from the power of death, and is the talisman of rebirth. Gawain's manner of receiving it was undoubtedly questionable. He accepted it with a pang of shame, surreptitiously, as booty snatched in secrecy and concealed. Had he been able to return it at the moment of the evening exchange, his initiation might have taken some less frightful form; he might have been spared the encounter at the Green Chapel. Nevertheless, after the completion of the trial there can be no doubt that he merits the trophy, and so Death settles it upon him as a legitimate gift.

In this late chivalric adventure Death plays the same role as in the ancient myths and epics of Gilgamesh, Herakles, Theseus and Orpheus. Those earlier heroes, too, went into the nether world (or into far-off, forbidden or unknown lands) to gain through death's mystery the treasure of everlasting life. But in the present version the point of the challenge, temptation, and trial, is not made quite clear. The romance seems to miss something of its own suggested depth. It does not insist upon its meaning. One cannot even be sure that the thirteenth and fourteenth century French and English poets, who constructed this romance out of earlier materials, consciously intended the reading that inevitably emerges when the traditional episodes which they successfully synthesized are comparatively construed. The Green Knight, for example, before dismissing Gawain, opens his visor and discloses his true face, his hidden character and significance; yet the name that he announces is not his true *nomen*. He introduces himself merely as *Bernlak de Hautdesert*, "Bernlak of the Lofty Desert." Still another joke of disguise, played this time not on the hero alone but on the readers and the poets too.

The imposing older matron within the castle is revealed to be Morgan the Fay, once the mistress of the wise and powerful Merlin, whose wizardry she learned and whom she then conjured into a living grave. It is declared that she was the one who had sent the Green Knight on his mission to King Arthur's court and by her magic had given him the power to play that trick with his head. One of her sons, it seems, had been refused admission to the exclusive circle of the Round Table, and being a revengeful woman she had wished to discredit the valor of the knights. She had also hoped that Queen Guinevere might drop dead of the fright and shame. She herself is the king's half-sister and therefore an aunt of Sir Gawain, who is King Arthur's nephew, etc., etc. It is apparent that the interest of the adventure has degenerated to the purely social and genealogical level. Themes that must once have been enacted on a higher mythical stage now appear obscured and encumbered with the trappings of chivalric pride and family intrigue. Indeed, such is the case with the whole cycle of Sir Gawain—not alone with this present encounter of the Green Knight. Gawain's numerous legends are alive with wonderful mythological images, adventures in lonely enchanted castles and on lovely far-off fairy isles, but all the mythology has become transformed according to the social formulae of medieval amour and knightly tournament. A watchful eye, nevertheless, can detect and read again the older symbolism with its timeless meaning.

E. Talbot Donaldson

It is possible that the plot of *Sir Gawain* came ready-made to the poet, who may have found it in some lost French poem or have heard it recited in English—perhaps even in Welsh—in his own country. The motif of the green man's decapitation originates in very ancient folklore, probably in a vegetation myth in which the beheading would have been a ritual death that insured the return of spring to the earth and the regrowth of the crops. But this primitive theme has been entirely rationalized by the late medieval poet, who sees in his inherited plot an opportunity to study how successfully Gawain, as a man wholly dedicated to Christian ideals, maintains those ideals when he is subjected to unusual pressures. The poem is a rare combination: at once a comedy—even a satire—of manners and a profoundly Christian view of man's character and his destiny. The court of King Arthur is presented, in the most grandiose and laudatory of language, as the place where the ideal of chivalry has reached its

Reprinted from The Norton Anthology of English Literature, *M. H. Abrams, General Editor, Vol. 1, pp. 183–84. By permission of W. W. Norton & Company, Inc. Copyright © 1962 by W. W. Norton & Company, Inc.*

zenith, where all is courtesy and martial prowess in defense of the right. The praise bestowed by the poet upon this court may seem excessive, and indeed the sequel suggests that the author made it so intentionally. For when the court is invaded by the Green Knight, arrogant, monstrous, and yet exasperatingly reasonable, it suddenly seems to become slightly unreal, as if, the Green Knight insultingly implies, its reputation were founded more on fiction than on fact—as if the poets that celebrated it had been working harder to enhance its glory than the knights themselves. In any case, the court is to receive a testing, which is naturally entrusted to the most courteous and valiant knight of the Round Table (in this most English of Arthurian romances Gawain has not been replaced as the best of knights by the continental-born Lancelot).

Once Gawain has set out to keep his promise to the Green Knight, his humiliation—and by inference that of the court—begins: in describing Gawain's adventures the poet, for all his epic enhancement and overt praise for the hero, actually tells a tale of his increasing helplessness. First of all Gawain's courtesy fails him—not, to be sure, in the sense that he relinquishes it, but in the sense that it involves him in a profoundly embarrassing and dangerous situation with the lady: it results in trouble instead of the serenity that courtesy, as the diplomat's virtue, is supposed to procure. Then the second of his great virtues, his martial prowess, is denied to him by the promise he has made not to defend himself against the Green Knight's return stroke. Thus betrayed by or cut off from the two qualities that he supposes to have made him the splendid knight people think him to be, he also, with very human lack of logic, momentarily cuts himself off from the power that has actually permitted those qualities to flourish in him. For when the pressures increase, St. Mary's knight, no longer able to rely on himself, relies not on St. Mary but on a belt of supposed magical powers, which he must accept from the lady with ignominy and hide from her lord with dishonesty. When the Green Knight spares his life there is revealed to Gawain his own real impoverishment, the complete incapacity of the greatest of Arthur's knights to help himself. He has found that without God's grace the virtues which he has made particularly his own are of no use to him —that, indeed, he no longer possesses them. The poem ends happily; but the baldric that the courtiers wear in honor of Gawain's adventure is a reminder that what God asks of men is not primarily courtly or martial prowess, but a humble and a contrite heart.

This didactic point is made with a most Chaucer-like indirection, a fine irony that strips Gawain of his pretensions but leaves him his charm and shows him sympathy for the really quite unfair nature of his predicament—and which also enjoys, and makes the reader enjoy, the embarrassment the hero is made to suffer. . . .

C. S. Lewis

It is not to be disputed that literary texts can sometimes be of great use to the anthropologist. It does not immediately follow from this that anthropological study can make in return any valuable contribution to literary criticism. The attention now paid by medievalists to the mythical and ritual origins (real or supposed) of the romances suggests a widespread belief that it can. I want to consider how far this is so. . . .

It has been maintained that Bercilak in *Gawain and the Green Knight* 'is'—that is, was influenced by—an *eniautos daimon*.[1] Let us suppose, for purposes of argument, that this is so. The question is which of the two, *eniautos daimon* or Bercilak, throws light on the other.

Bercilak is as vivid and concrete as any image I have met in literature. He is a living *coincidentia oppositorum;* half giant, yet wholly a 'lovely knight'; as full of demoniac energy as old Karamazov, yet, in his own house, as jolly as a Dickensian Christmas host; now exhibiting a ferocity so gleeful that it is almost genial, and now a geniality so outrageous that it borders on the ferocious; half boy or buffoon in his shouts and laughter and jumpings; yet at the end judging Gawain with the tranquil superiority of an angelic being. There has been nothing really like him in fiction before or since. No one who has once read the poem forgets him. No one while reading it disbelieves in him.

But what is the *eniautos daimon?* It is a concept; something con-

---

From "The Anthropological Approach" by C. S. Lewis, in English and Medieval Studies Presented to J. R. R. Tolkien on the Occasion of his Seventieth Birthday, *eds. Norman Davis and C. L. Wrenn (London: George Allen & Unwin, Ltd., 1962), pp. 219, 222–23. Copyright © 1962 by George Allen & Unwin, Ltd. Reprinted by permission of the publisher.*

[1] [Literally, a year or anniversary daemon: see pp. 95–98 above—Ed.]

structed from the actual practices of the ancient world and the conjectured practices of our own ancestors. I have never seen Jack in the Green. None of us have, as believers, taken part in a pagan ritual. We cannot experience such things from inside. We may sometimes know, and sometimes guess, that certain myths were told and certain rites enacted. We do not know what it felt like. That world-old religion, with its baffling mixture of agriculture, tragedy, obscenity, revelry, and clowning, eludes us in all but its externals.

To expect that the *eniautos daimon* should help us to understand Bercilak is to expect that the unknown should illuminate the known; as if we hoped that a man would learn more about the taste of oranges on being told that it is like the taste of some other fruit which he has never eaten.

The opposite process is the only rational one. Tell me that the unknown fruit is like an orange, and I have learned something. I learn nothing about the quality of Bercilak from being told he is derived from the daimon; I may learn something about the daimon. Perhaps this rumbustious, irresistible figure has preserved for me just what anthropology can never penetrate; has given me knowledge-by-acquaintance (*connaître*) where anthropology could give me at best knowledge-about (*savoir*). If this is so, then our poetic experience has helped us as anthropologists, but our anthropology has not helped us to read the poetry. When savage beliefs or practices inform a work of art, that work is not a puzzle to which those beliefs and practices are the clue. The savage origins are the puzzle; the surviving work of art is the only clue by which we can hope to penetrate the inwardness of the origins. It is either in art, or nowhere, that the dry bones are made to live again.

A. C. Spearing

In *Sir Gawain and the Green Knight*, finally, we have moved considerably further than in *Pearl* away from a direct confrontation between man and God. Gawain, as the chosen representative of the

From "Patience and the Gawain-Poet" *by A. C. Spearing, in* Anglia, Vol. 84 *(Tübingen: Max Niemeyer Verlag, 1966), 325–29. Copyright © 1966 by Max Niemeyer Verlag. Reprinted by permission of the author and the publisher. The original footnotes have been omitted, and translations have been supplied.*

Arthurian civilization, takes up a challenge offered by the Green
Knight, and the Green Knight is a figure whose power is clear, but
whose theological or metaphysical status is completely uncertain. At
one point it is strongly hinted that he may be a devil; at another he
assumes the role of a Christian priest. His own explanation of the
test to which he submits Camelot is in terms of a vaguely defined
magic, and it has, I think, been generally felt by modern readers that
it does not do much to explain what is actually in the poem. Mr.
John Speirs writes of it as "a bone for the rationalizing mind to play
with," and I rejoice to concur with him. Indeed, a mystery surrounding the Green Knight is essential for the effect of the poem, which is
to show Gawain being submitted to the unexpected—not to the test
he expects, but to one he does not expect. He expects (and we expect with him when we first read the poem) that the real test he has to
nerve himself for is meeting the Green Knight at the Green Chapel
and receiving a presumably mortal blow from his axe. But when,
after a tremendous effort of will, he does bring himself to face the
Green Knight and accept the blow, it turns out that this is not the
test itself; it is only the symbol of a previous test which was carried
out by the Green Knight's wife, and which Gawain has already failed.
The same pattern occurs too in Gawain's confrontation with the wife
in the castle: she conducts a wily and determined assault on his chastity, which he eventually resists, only to succumb, after this soften-
ing-up process, to what seems a much more minor temptation, the
acceptance and concealment of her girdle, which she says will protect
him from the axe-blow. From this way of looking at it, I think it will
be clear that the situations in which Gawain finds himself make it
extremely difficult for him to retain his dignity, let alone any heroic
quality. At the beginning of the poem, he is a genuinely glamorous
figure, far more so than the formal heroes of the other poems in the
manuscript, and he sets out on what appears to be a genuinely heroic
adventure, in which he will die rather than let himself and Camelot
be dishonored. He never completely loses this heroic quality, but as
he progresses on his adventure he is forced into less and less heroic
situations, and is submitted to a more and more detailed and realistic
psychological appraisal. The result is that our picture of Gawain becomes increasingly tinged with a comedy that diminishes his stature.

   This is particularly the effect of the scenes with the lady, the wife
of the Green Knight in his role as Sir Bertilak. The *Joseph Andrews*-
like comic potential of the reversal of the sexual roles that takes place

between them is obvious: he defending his chastity against her clever
and varied attack, abetted as it is from within himself both by his
natural desire and by the second nature of his famous *cortaysye*. She
hunts him as her husband hunts the wild animals; and the brilliant
and subtle comedy of these three bedroom scenes has been so generally recognized that it needs no elaboration here. In a kind of symbolic unchastity, he finally accepts the life-saving girdle from her and
conceals it from her husband. When he resumes his quest for the
Green Chapel and leaves the luxurious castle behind there is room
once more for heroism in his behavior, and indeed he shows heroism
of a particularly touching kind—not the kind that knows no fear,
but the kind that overcomes a fear to which all the senses are sharp-
ened. He proudly turns aside the suggestion of his guide that he
should go back to Camelot, and nobody would know that he had not
faced the Green Knight, saying that if he did that, even though nobody found out, he would still be a "knyȝt kowarde" (2131). Yet
even this heroism is tainted by our knowledge that he possesses the
girdle, and at least hopes it will save him. The moment of his arrival
at the Green Chapel is very finely done, the tension being wound up
in a deliberate way that once again makes us accomplices with the
poet. Gawain hears the sudden noise of grinding—as if someone were
sharpening a scythe—and then screws himself up to call out his
challenge:

> Who stiȝtleȝ in þis sted me steuen to holde?
> For now is gode Gawayn goande ryȝt here.
> If any wyȝe oȝt wyl, wynne hider fast,
> Oþer now oþer neuer, his nedeȝ to spede.

(2213–6)

[Who is master in this place, to keep tryst with me? For now is good
Gawain walking right here. If any man wishes anything, let him come
here quickly, either now or never, to further his needs.]

The movement of the verse seems to impose a quiver on one's voice
as one reads this courageous shout, and the implication of the emphasis on speed is very plain: now or never, if the challenger fails to
keep his appointment on the instant, Gawain will feel justified in
being off. The answer, significantly, is "Abyde" (2217). Who can
blame Gawain? On the contrary, we feel for him most sympathetically;
but there is no denying that we are also amused by his predicament.
There is a further winding up of tension in the actual meeting of

the two opponents. First Gawain ducks as he sees the axe descending on him; then the Green Knight deliberately feints at him to test his courage; finally he strikes a slight blow, and, as Gawain leaps up in relief, stands aside and explains that the three strokes represent the three days' temptation in the castle. Gawain is full of anger and shame; he throws down the girdle, and, a little later, raves uncontrollably against the wiles of women, his *cortaysye* quite abandoned. For a moment, when the Green Knight stands aside, we see Gawain through his eyes; and this is so rare an event in the poem that the situation is peculiarly memorable. He is pleased with him, as one might be pleased with a child or a pet animal that showed fighting spirit. His first words are: "Bolde burne, on þis bent be not so gryndel" (2338), and they strikingly echo the advice that God gives to Jonah at the end of *Patience*:

> Be noȝt so gryndel, Godman, bot go forth þy wayes:
> Be preue & be pacient in payne & in joye . . .

(524–5)

[Be not so fierce, good man, but go on your way: be brave and be patient in pain and in joy . . .]

One might well ask, what else could Gawain do? The very plot of the poem has conspired against him, to turn the game that the Green Knight originally suggested into deadly earnest, and then to turn the earnest into game again, a joke of which Gawain is the butt after all. To be the victim of a trick is perhaps the worst blow Gawain has to endure, because it deprives him of his self-esteem.

The end of the poem is enigmatic, and I think intentionally so. Through most of the story we have been very close to Gawain, seeing through his eyes, and possessing a privileged access to his very stream of consciousness. But towards the end the poet draws away from Gawain without coming closer to any of the other characters. He tells us simply what happened: Gawain told his story, the courtiers laughed, they adopted the green girdle as a badge of honor. One would like very much to know the meaning of their laughter, and the nature of Gawain's reaction to it; but the poet keeps his silence, and the story at last recedes into the legendary history from which it emerged. We are left with food for much discussion as to the proper attitude to be adopted towards Gawain's experience. What is firm and real in the poem is the experience itself, both physical and moral:

the valiant but eventually hopeless struggle against a power beyond the natural, which tests men, searches out their imperfections, and at last, most devastating of all to the heroic aspiration, forgives them.

Cecily Clark

The Lady, then, is given her own characteristic voice: a variable voice, admittedly, sometimes marked by breaks of syntax and shifts of tone, at others more disciplined, but always complex and nuanced and slyly building up suspense in the hearer's mind—though no more variable, certainly, than that of any real person. Apart from the minor point concerning pronouns of address, her style bears no resemblance to her husband's: whereas his speeches are almost devoid of conditional elements, these are just what hers abound in, being one of the chief means by which delay and suspense are achieved; and, although she may now and then throw out an imperative ('*Dos teches* me of your wytte . . .'), her normal address is much more indirect than his. This indirect and shifting manner is appropriate to the disingenuous rôle she is playing, and her use of suspense enhances her temptations.

Moreover, there is yet a more subtle way in which the Lady's style is adapted to the rôle she plays, for, as we have already observed, it is indeed Gawain's usage which hers most closely resembles. The two styles are not identical (it would be a considerable blemish in the poem if they were), but to serve their different ends they use much of the same syntactical devices, 'qualifications and delays'. And this is dramatically satisfying. In analysing the Guide's temptation of Gawain we noted that the alien idiom in which this is expressed seems to make it easier and more natural for Gawain to reject it. With the Lady it is just the reverse: the speech-patterns (and therefore the thought-patterns) with which she assails Gawain are very like his own, so that at its most persuasive her voice must seem to him to be saying things he might have thought himself. It is natural and dramatically right therefore that this temptation proffered in his own complex idiom should be the one to which Gawain succumbs.

From "Sir Gawain and the Green Knight: Characterisation by Syntax" by Cecily Clark, in Essays in Criticism, *Vol. XVI (1966), 372–74. Copyright © 1966 by Essays in Criticism. Reprinted by permission of F. W. Bateson.*

Even an analysis as brief and incomplete as this makes it clear how each of the characters in *Sir Gawain and the Green Knight* is given an individual voice and how the chief means of differentiating these voices is variation in syntax. This is particularly effective as a means of characterisation, since of all the elements of language syntax is the one which most readily creates the illusion of reflecting the inner workings of the mind. Not, of course, that the poet himself would have formulated his method in any such terms: he no doubt worked by intuition based on observation of how differences in linguistic habit often reflect differences in personality (do we not all know living speakers who combine the Green Knight's fondness for unqualified imperatives with his domineering attitude to his fellow-men?). In any event, for a poet working within the conventions of alliterative verse it was a brilliant stroke to choose syntax as the instrument of characterisation, for in this medium syntax is the linguistic feature most readily varied, vocabulary and phraseology being necessarily so much subject to the exigencies of the meter. And this is not all; for, not content with inventing distinctive voices for each main character, the poet has so tuned and modulated those voices as to make them echo, contrast and counterpoint one another in as it were an orchestration of character.

Ralph W. V. Elliott

One day in May, 1135, some white monks from Combermere Abbey founded a new Cistercian monastery near a ford of the Dee at Poulton a few miles upstream from Chester. In itself this was no very epoch-making event, but evidence is accumulating to strengthen the view that in due course the founding of Poulton Abbey led to the writing of the greatest medieval English poem outside the work of Chaucer: *Sir Gawain and the Green Knight*.

The poet has left us no clue to his identity or habitat except the sensuous vividness of his landscape painting, which suggests both a remarkable eye for detail and a close familiarity with the scenes depicted, and at one place in the poem, while Sir Gawain searches

---

"Sir Gawain in Staffordshire: A Detective Essay in Literary Geography" by Ralph W. V. Elliott, London Times, *May 21, 1958, p. 12. Reprinted by permission of the London* Times.

for the Green Chapel, we are actually given a piece of genuine itinerary. Sir Gawain is journeying through North Wales, leaving Anglesey on his left hand, and then crosses the Dee by some ford into the "wilderness of Wirral."

The remaining action of the poem takes place in or near the castle of Bercilak de Hautdesert (who later turns out to be the Green Knight) and, although no more place-names are mentioned, the poet was obviously at home in the wild, hilly countryside he describes. The nearest scenery fitting these descriptions within the area covered by the poet's dialect is the Staffordshire Peak country, and here is our first important link with Poulton, for as the Welsh proved unruly neighbors, the whole abbey, while retaining its Cheshire possessions, was transplanted, in May, 1214, to a wild corner of North Stafford-shire moorland, by the river Churnet near Leek, to become the abbey of St. Mary and St. Benedict of Dieulacres.

The organizer of this move was Ranulph, Earl of Chester, whose father according to tradition had died near the same spot, at his favorite hunting lodge of Swythamley, which formed part of the new abbey's endowment. Here the monks established one of their granges, half farm, half miniature monastery, cultivating forest and marsh until the grange became the "Parke-laund" of the sixteenth century, and it is still a private seat.

There was never a castle at Swythamley such as Sir Gawain so opportunely discovered, but not only is Gawain's approach to the castle very like the journey from the present Abbey Farm (with its few pathetic remains of the monastic buildings) to Swythamley Park, but there is also a distinct likeness between the terrain at Swythamley with its central eminence, once called Knight's Low, and the situation of the poetic castle, enthroned *on a lawe*. That such a castle never actually existed need not surprise us, for the several up-to-date features so expertly enumerated by the poet were only just beginning to make their separate appearance in English domestic and ecclesiastical architecture. It was a brilliant vision superimposed upon a genuine English hill.

It is here that Sir Gawain relaxes and is subjected to the temptation of his alluring hostess while her husband is away hunting, for three successive days, deer, boar, and fox. Here again the terrain is at times so vividly described that identification becomes possible, particularly on the second day, that of the boar hunt.

Starting from Swythamley, within echoing distance of the Roaches (the poet's *rocheres*), the hunters crossed the latter then headed northwards past Flash (the poet's *flosche*) towards the steep banks and narrow valleys of the Wildboarclough country beyond the river Dane. Many of the features the poet mentions in unusual topographical words still bear the same or closely similar names to-day.

Sir Gawain was able to relax at Bercilak's castle because upon arrival he had been assured that the Green Chapel which he sought was "not two miles hence." Again the poet was speaking from personal knowledge, and it is almost uncanny to read his description and the directions given to Gawain by his guide and then to walk the two miles that separate Swythamley Park from what is surely one of the most fantastic natural chapels in existence. From the top of a "high hill" Gawain's guide points to a steep valley:—

> Ride down this path along that rocky bank
> Till you reach the bottom of this forbidding valley,
> Then look up a little among the trees on your left hand,
> And there, along the valley, you will see the Green Chapel.

Anyone can make the same journey to-day, first climbing up towards Roach End from Swythamley, then turning sharply northwards and down again, steeply, some 500 feet in under a mile, into the valley of the Black Brook and thus to its junction with the Dane at the Forest Bottom. Sir Gawain saw no building there, only rocky crags and strange piles of stones all *knokled* and *knorned;* and indeed all you can see to-day, up on the left bank, are the twisted shapes of the Castle Cliff Rocks.

But the poet knew that there was something else there, "either an old cave or a crevice of an old crag—he could not say for certain," a tremendous rock fissure entered through a cave-like hole in the hillside. Already in the seventeenth century Dr. Plot, historian of Staffordshire, knew it as Lud's Church or Ludchurch, truly a weird church, about 100 ft. long, with vertical walls up to over 50 ft. high, nowhere above 10 ft. wide, and with a hole at each end leading downwards into the earth and hitherto only partly explored. Tradition records it as the hiding place of Lollards and the surrounding region is rich with legends of headless riders and a tall man in Lincoln green.

One other detail the poet adds, and again its source is at the same spot: after Sir Gawain has climbed to the top of the Green Chapel he hears from "that high hill" a strange tumult emanating from the

other side of the brook, a fierce grinding noise "grievous to hear."
There is no forge now at the Forest Bottom, but on old maps it is
still marked, and the little wooden bridge over the Black Brook still
bears the revealing name of the original stone arch, Castor's Bridge,
and traces of iron slag lie not far below the soil. That the Cistercians
of Dieulacres and Swythamley grange worked this forge has yet to be
proved, but it is highly probable.

Other interesting links remain to strengthen the chain of evidence
that connects Poulton and Dieulacres with *Sir Gawain and the Green
Knight*; it is hoped to publish them before long. Not the least remarkable of them is the fact that just when the poet was combining,
for the first time, it is believed, in English his two themes of the
temptation of Gawain and the beheading challenge, the abbot of
Dieulacres was involved in 1379 in a very shady incident in which a
local man of some substance was beheaded on the moors just outside
Leek.

By themselves these parallels and identifications may not amount to
much, but added up they present a body of evidence which may
bring us closer than ever before to this unknown artist of the fourteenth century. It is no wasted labor, for he was a great English poet.

Chronology of Important Dates

c. 500	The battle of *Mons Badonicus,* in which the (Celtic) Britons defeated the Saxons. The historical Arthur (if he existed at all) may have been the commander of the Britons.
c. 1135	Geoffrey of Monmouth's *Historia Regum Britanniae,* a legendary history of the Britons. The fundamental source for many of the Arthurian legends.
c. 1155	Wace's *Roman de Brut,* an Anglo-Norman paraphrase of Geoffrey's *Historia.*
1170–90	The Arthurian romances of Chrétien de Troyes.
c. 1200	Layamon's *Brut,* a Middle English paraphrase of Wace's *Roman de Brut.*
c. 1360	The alliterative *Morte Arthure.*
1360–1400	*Sir Gawain and the Green Knight, Pearl, Patience, Purity; Piers Plowman.*
1377–99	Reign of Richard II.
c. 1390	Gower's *Confessio Amantis.*
1399	Death of John of Gaunt, Duke of Lancaster.
1400	Chaucer's death.
1485	Caxton's publication of Malory's *Le Morte Darthur.*
1839	First publication of *Sir Gawain and the Green Knight.*

Notes on the Editor and Contributors

DENTON FOX, the editor of this anthology, is an Associate Professor at Victoria College, University of Toronto, where he teaches Old and Middle English.

LARRY BENSON, the author of *Art and Tradition in Sir Gawain and the Green Knight* (1965), teaches at Harvard, and has written on many aspects of Old and Middle English literature.

MARIE BORROFF, Professor of English at Yale, has published her own poetry, as well as scholarly studies of Middle English and modern verse. All of these interests are reflected in her recent translation of *Gawain* (1967).

JOHN BURROW, Fellow and Librarian of Jesus College, Oxford, has written many articles on Old and Middle English literature, as well as *A Reading of Sir Gawain and the Green Knight* (1965).

CECILY CLARK, who has taught at the Universities of Edinburgh and of Aberdeen, is now living in Cambridge, where she is attached to Newnham College. She has published a number of articles on medieval literature.

E. TALBOT DONALDSON, now Professor of English at Columbia, has been directly or indirectly responsible for much of the best recent criticism of medieval English literature.

R. W. V. ELLIOTT was born in Berlin, educated in Scotland, and is now Professor of English in the Flinders University of South Australia. He has written extensively on both modern and medieval literature.

DOROTHY EVERETT, the first holder of the Readership in English Language at Oxford, died in 1953. She intended the selection included here to be part of a volume on Middle English Literature before Chaucer for the Oxford History of English Literature, a volume which she did not live to complete.

DONALD HOWARD, Professor of English at Johns Hopkins, has recently published *The Three Temptations: Medieval Man in Search of the World* (1966), a work which deals with *Piers Plowman* and *Troilus and Criseyde* as well as with *Gawain*.

C. S. Lewis, who died in 1963, was one of the most influential critics of this century, as well as a prolific novelist and Christian apologist. Among his best known critical works are *The Allegory of Love* (1936) and *English Literature in the Sixteenth Century* (Oxford History of English Literature, 1954).

Gervase Mathew, o.p., has lectured for many years in the English and History Faculties at Oxford, and has written on church history, Byzantine art and aesthetics, and African history. His new book, *The Court of Richard II* (1968), is of great interest for students of Gawain and other late-fourteenth-century literature.

A. C. Spearing is a Fellow of Queens' College, Cambridge. Some of his work on *Gawain*, *Piers Plowman*, and Chaucer is included in his recent *Criticism and Medieval Poetry* (1964).

John Speirs is Professor of English at the University of Exeter. His best known works include *The Scots Literary Tradition* (1940), *Chaucer the Maker* (1951), and *Medieval English Poetry: The Non-Chaucerian Tradition* (1957).

B. J. Whiting, Professor of English at Harvard, has written extensively on proverbs, folklore, and many aspects of medieval literature.

Heinrich Zimmer, who died in 1943, was a distinguished student of Indian mythology and symbolism. *The King and the Corpse* (1948), from which the selection in this volume is taken, was published posthumously after being revised by Joseph Campbell.

Selected Bibliography

There have been two important scholarly editions of *Sir Gawain and the Green Knight*, one edited by Sir Israel Gollancz, Mabel Day, and Mary S. Serjeantson, Early English Text Society, Original Series, No. 210 (London: Oxford University Press, 1940); the other edited by J. R. R. Tolkien and E. V. Gordon (Oxford: Clarendon Press, 1925). A second edition of the latter work has just appeared, revised by Norman Davis (Oxford: Clarendon Press, 1967); this volume incorporates much of the recent scholarship on the poem, and will presumably be accepted as the standard edition. But a beginner will find the poem easier to read in the volume edited by A. C. Cawley, *Pearl and Sir Gawain and the Green Knight* (London: Everyman's Library, 1962), which has marginal glosses and footnote paraphrases. Marie Borroff's translation (New York: W. W. Norton and Company, Inc., 1967) is in all ways superior to the numerous earlier translations.

The two best general books on *Gawain* are J. A. Burrow, *A Reading of Sir Gawain and the Green Knight* (London: Routledge & Kegan Paul, 1965), and Larry D. Benson, *Art and Tradition in Sir Gawain and the Green Knight* (New Brunswick, N. J.: Rutgers University Press, 1965). These books are also useful for bibliography, while a valuable survey of the scholarship on the poem up to 1960 is provided by Morton W. Bloomfield in *"Sir Gawain and the Green Knight: An Appraisal,"* PMLA, LXXVI (1961), 7–19. Two interesting articles on special topics are Derek A. Pearsall, "Rhetorical 'Descriptio' in 'Sir Gawain and the Green Knight,' " *Modern Language Review*, L (1955), 129–34, and Elizabeth Salter, "The Alliterative Revival. II," *Modern Philology*, LXIV (1967), 233–37 (a discussion of the social background of the Gawain-poet). A general account of the Arthurian background is given in *Arthurian Literature in the Middle Ages: A Collaborative History*, ed. R. S. Loomis (Oxford: Clarendon Press, 1959); see the chapter by R. W. Ackerman for a description of the other Middle English poems on Gawain.

TWENTIETH CENTURY VIEWS

British Authors